THE REIKI HANDBOOK

A Manual for Students and Therapists
of the Usui Shiko Ryoho System of Healing

BY

LARRY E. ARNOLD AND SANDRA K. NEVIUS

PSI Press
ParaScience International
1025 Miller Lane
Harrisburg, PA 17110-2899
1982

"For we in medicine are on the threshold of once again realizing that there are far greater powers at work in the minds and bodies of our patients and ourselves than we can understand or control by 'technical' means alone."

— Dr. Michael L. Connell,
"Spirit, Soul . . . and Medicine"
Unity, July 1979, 27.

ISBN 0-9625500-1-9

For information, write PSI Press, 1025 Miller Lane, Harrisburg, PA 17110-2899

First Edition June 1982
Second edition June 1985
Third printing March 1986   Fourth printing February 1987
Fifth printing September 1987   Sixth printing May 1988   Seventh printing February 1989
Third Edition January 1990
Ninth printing July 1990   Tenth printing January 1991   Eleventh printing August 1991
Twelfth printing March 1992   Thirteenth printing August 1992
Fourth Edition November 1992
Fifteenth printing July 1993   Sixteenth printing March 1994   Seventeenth printing July 1994
Eighteenth printing January 1995   Nineteenth printing May 1995   Twentieth printing January 1996
Twenty-first printing June 1996   Twenty-second printing December 1996   Twenty-third printing May 1997
Twenty-fourth printing December 1997   Twenty-fifth printing June 1998   Twenty-sixth printing March 1999
Twenty-seventh printing September 1999   Twenty-eight printing April 2000   Twenty-ninth printing October 2000
Thirtieth printing April 2001   Thirty-first printing Sept. 2001   Thirty-second printing April 2002
Thirty-third printing March 2003
Thirty-fourth printing April 2004

dedicated to

Dr. Mikao Usui

and

all who seek to restore balance
to the life-forms of this world

"We are the curators of life on earth. It is our birthright." — Dr. Helen Caldicott

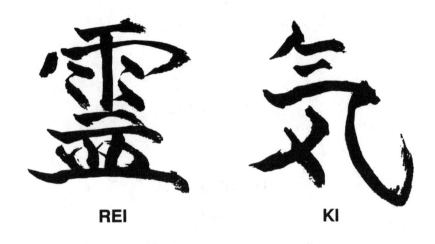

REI   **KI**

Rei means "spirit" or "soul". Esoterically it conveys supernatural knowledge or spiritual consciousness, and awareness of and ability to work within that greater wisdom.

Ki means "energy" and originally connoted a sense of air or atmosphere; that which pervades and surrounds. Ki is the life force, in its many variants.

These Japanese *kanji*, or ideograms, combine as Reiki to embody the concept of a universal life force appropriate to healing — a spiritually guided, all-enveloping energy of the body, soul and spirit.

Table of Contents

Preface

The authors received their first-degree Reiki certification under the tutorage of Reiki Master Virginia W. Samdahl in August, 1981, at the Spiritual Frontiers Fellowship Southeastern Retreat in Greensboro, North Carolina.

During that time in which a deep respect and friendship developed with this dynamic lady of simple sincerity and unassailable conviction in the validity and value of the Reiki system, there also was fostered the idea of a thorough manual that could assist the student of Reiki to more easily learn — and subsequently apply more effectively — this very ancient yet only recently rediscovered art of natural healing.

As you certainly know, in most learning exercises a good teacher has a lot of important knowledge to present — to which the student responds by attempting to absorb *all* of it — in a very limited amount of time. This situation was immediately encountered with Mrs. Samdahl, as it undoubtedly is with any of the Reiki master teachers.

Inevitably the student is at the disadvantage, because to him or her the material is new. And since the teacher probably won't be around to clarify a missed point one week after the course, usually the student compounds his dilemma by frantically trying to take detailed notes — which invariably results in consciously missing (either not seeing or hearing or correctly recording) important information.

Magnifying this dilemma for the authors (and other participants in the Retreat workshop) was the fact Mrs. Samdahl spoke very rapidly — a factor not at all uncommon in those enthusiastic about their work. Those who didn't know shorthand were quickly at a further disadvantage, soon developing writer's cramp. That's when tape recorders began to appear ... which helped only those who had fortuitously brought theirs to the Retreat.

But while taping is great for straight lecturing, it's less than ideal when lecturing is intimately linked to hands-on instruction. The solution would have been for each student to have a basic pictorial manual designed to complement the teacher's instruction, in which the student could highlight points emphasized by the teacher and quickly add personal notes for later referral.

Except that such a reference manual didn't exist. Thus was born the idea for *The Reiki Handbook*.

The *Handbook* is structured to parallel the standard format for Reiki certification: the story of the rediscovery by Dr. Usui of an ancient healing process in the venerable sutras, the principles of the Reiki system of natural healing, the Whole Body treatment positions as handed down by Dr. Usui, along with additional processes and resource information that would be useful to the individual who wishes to actively employ Reiki in his life and to the life around him.

The one major aspect of the Reiki system not covered by the *Handbook* is the transmission of the Reiki energy from the master to the student. That, and the innate understanding, warmth and vitality which the Reiki master herself (or himself) naturally brings to the student.

As such, it must be clear that the *Handbook* is not — nor should it be perceived as — intended to supplant the master's role in the Reiki system. It cannot. Rather, the *Handbook* is designed as a practical workbook so that the student, freed from the undue distraction of massive note-taking, can more effectively benefit from the special insights to be garnered from personal contact with the Reiki master. Instruction time and attention can then focus on hand placements and recognizing the subtle energy changes that manifest during Reiki transfers and healing.

We hope *The Reiki Handbook* serves you well, now as a student and in the future as a reference manual, as you become attuned to and channel the "health through hands" that Reiki offers.

Credits

A book of this nature results from the cooperation of many individuals, generously sharing their talents and expertise. The authors wish to show their appreciation for this assistance by gratefully acknowledging their contributions.

Photography: Jack Miller and Larry Arnold, with additional photo credits to Virginia Samdahl.

Modeling for the Reiki atlas: Linda Linder and John O'Brien.

Cover design: Samantha Groom and Larry Arnold. General book design and layout by North Mountain Artisans. Rear cover art of "Phyltoslachys heterocycla" from A. B. Freeman-Mitford's *The Bamboo Garden* (1896).

General support or technical assistance: Dorothy Buba, John Burkholder, Barbara Jean Cashman, Reiki Master Nonie Greene, Reiki Master David Jarrell, Richard and Jane Neff, Tomoko Nonaka, Yonnie Wells, Jitsuro Yamamoto, and Dr. Lewis Hartman. Plus Jeanne Barbara Cluny, for gracious permission to publish "The Subconscious Nature of Healing."

Particular mention is due Reiki Master Virginia Samdahl, who checked the accuracy of and contributed extensive commentary on the manuscript as well as furnishing the authors with rare and personal resource materials. She also arranged the final photo sessions that assured the pictorial accuracy of the Reiki atlas. Without her invaluable support and backing from its inception to completion, *The Reiki Handbook* would be less than it is.

"Socrates reported to his Greek countrymen that in one respect the Barbarian Tracians were in advance of civilization. They knew the body could not be cured without the mind. This is the reason why the cure of many diseases is unknown to the physicians of Hellas, because they are ignorant of the whole."

—Dr. H. F. Dunbar, in his essay *Emotions and Bodily Change* to the College of Physicians, Philadelphia, PA; March 15, 1951.

Introduction

Man's natural state is one of health.

Ironically few people seem to enjoy, or be blessed with, a life of physical well-being. Dis-ease, sickness or injury becomes a chosen experience in almost everyone's life; in fact, the more some people suffer the more they seem to delight in their imbalance.

Yet exceptionally rare is the person who doesn't express the desire to be free of disease, the more quickly the better!

Therefore, health — and subsequently healing — are major topics of human discussion and exploration.

Not surprisingly in Age of Consciousness groups there is much emphasis on healing, especially forms labeled "nontraditional" or "natural" that circumvent or are alleged to lessen the need for the myriad drugs and surgical procedures that characterize modern medical science.

Elaborate arcane rituals and philosophical regimens are sometimes concocted — which may or may not have validity — that must be rigidly followed if the initiate can expect to be healed or function as a channel for healing energies.

With so many varieties of esoteric healing systems being touted, the field of nontraditional healing can easily be perceived as cultic, each system having its own idiosyncrasies or ideology that makes it unique and perhaps superior — despite the almost universal claim that the energy of healing flows from just one creative Source.

Is Reiki, then, anything other than one more candidate in this parade of paranormal healing systems? And, perhaps worse, a sort of metaphysical placebo hiding behind a false facade of elaborate mechanics offering no practical effectiveness? As one of the authors, Sandy, once said: "I felt Reiki was just another form of healing. I wasn't impressed."

Several friends of the authors were (and are) deeply involved in Reiki, however, and *praised* its results. Were they all deluding themselves? That was most unlikely. Yet obviously other healing systems seemed valid, too. What, if anything, set Reiki apart as a truly valuable process?

The answer could only be found in first-hand experience.

So while we both have been said to have an inborn "healing touch," when a special opportunity presented itself to take the Reiki certification we enrolled together, each with a skeptically open-minded attitude. After all, there was this mysterious "power transfer" that had to be done by an initiated Master teacher — and for pragmatists that disquietingly paralleled the basis for many nonconstructive cults.

True, there *was* a series of "power transfers" administered by the Reiki teacher, who had previously received special power transfers and advanced training from a descendant in the line of Grand Masters from Reiki's rediscoverer and thus was certified a Reiki Master. Just as conspicuous, though, by its *absence* was any attempt by the teacher to indoctrinate ... or brainwash ... the students into renouncing their own belief systems and subjugating themselves to the "one-and-only-way" of Reiki.

Cultism certainly wasn't an issue. What *was* at issue was healing.

For Sandy, she changed her assessment about Reiki. "It works!" she says simply. "It's easy. Not a lot of hoopla about technique, altering your state of consciousness, and all that. It produces results, fast!"

For the other author, proof of its efficacy came swiftly.

Four days after completing the Reiki course, and being certified in first-degree Reiki, both authors were deep in the Great Smoky Mountains on a nature hike guided by a U. S. National Park ranger. Suddenly in the middle of the verdant forest trail a searing pain stabbed Larry's left wrist. Oddly, he noticed, no one in the group around him seemed likewise affected.

Then he discovered why. An unseen bee, probably a hornet, had singled him out for attack — for firmly embedded in his wrist was a bee stinger, the swollen venom sack still attached.

The situation had all the elements of catastrophe. Bee venom is generally very toxic to Larry's body, causing extreme swelling and even temporary paralysis of limbs. There was more than a mile to hike before the trail exited the forest, and the unavoidable exertion could only hasten the spread of the toxin. Already in the few seconds since being stung, the forearm was turning red and swelling. Driving the car would be impossible, it seemed, and, since Sandy prefers not to drive at night, the future should have held a ruined vacation and a long painful trip home.

"But we've just been trained in Reiki," Larry thought. "Here's a test to see if it *really* works!"

Already he had removed the stinger and began sucking on the wound — an automatic reflex in keeping with the Reiki premise that saliva is healing.[1] After a few seconds, he cupped his right hand around the inflamed injury, as Sandy and John O'Brien, a traveling companion who had received Reiki certification along with the authors, came up the trail to see what was wrong.

The predicament explained, Sandy placed both her hands around the sting and John covered the forearm with his hands.

By this time the Park ranger walked up, and said that bee sting ointment was available at the Visitor's Center — more than a mile away through the forest.

Larry thanked him, and confidently said it wouldn't be needed. "We're doing Reiki."

"What's that?" quizzically asked the ranger. "You folks into something *occult?*"

For much of the rest of the hike, conversation focused on Reiki ... and topics related to Age of Consciousness thinking about the holism of life that Smoky Mountain National Park rangers apparently don't encounter very often in their tours — even though surrounded by the magnificence of an ecosystem whose healthy balance their work helps maintain.

For a while the pain of the sting subsided ... then intensified. According to

Reiki, this was to be expected: a temporary re-experiencing of the initial trauma as the body moved through it on the path to dismissing the injury entirely. Or was Reiki simply failing?

By the time the Visitor's Center was reached, the swelling which normally would have paralyzed Larry's arm was barely perceptible around the area of the sting itself. The ranger again offered to get his ointment, but by now it clearly wasn't necessary. We thanked him for his concern and the knowledge he shared about the nature in the forest around us. He thanked us for a nature talk of a different kind — about healing and metaphysics and "all that sort of stuff."

Treatment by Sandy and John continued for another 15 minutes in the quiet of a shaded glen in the southern Appalachian Mountains, and that was enough.

The swelling and pain were gone; paralysis never set in. The car could be driven as if nothing potentially catastrophic had ever happened. Reiki had rescued the vacation.

Reiki proved itself to the authors to be not only effective, but useful under conditions that would be untenable to many of the other nontraditional healing systems. Reiki worked, simply and beautifully.

Partially as a result of this experience, the authors committed themselves to writing this book.

And also as a result of this experience, perhaps someday Reiki will be incorporated in the U. S. National Park Service's emergency medical training because one of their rangers saw how easily and unpretentiously this natural healing system works.

Larry E. Arnold
Sandra K. Nevius

May 1982   Harrisburg, Pennsylvania

---

[1] Biochemical properties in saliva conducive to healing were confirmed by scientists in mid-1981. On September 9, 1992, Dr. David Mahamud announced that saliva clots blood and may even help arrest the transmission of AIDS and herpes: "Normally saliva is controlling these infections ..."

THE REIKI HANDBOOK

1

The Reiki Story

(AS TOLD BY VIRGINIA SAMDAHL)

A man named Mikao Usui, a very common name in Japan, was president and minister of the Christian School in Kyoto, Japan.

One morning after the message, some of his young graduating seniors came forward and said to him, "Dr. Usui sansei, we would like to ask you a question."

He said, "Gentlemen — "

And they said, "Sir, we would like to know whether or not you *really* understand what it says in the Bible — or if you just accept it on blind faith."

And he said, "I think I really understand what it says in the Bible."

And they said, "Oh, that's wonderful! We were hoping you would say that. If you really understand, we want you to do for us just one miracle. We don't care

what it is. We don't care if you walk on the water, if you make the deaf to hear, or the blind to see. We don't care. Just one miracle, if you truly understand what it says in the Bible!"

And he said, "Well I'm not sure, gentlemen, if I understand it in that way."

And they said, "But sir, we are graduating! And the charge is to go forth and preach and teach and heal the sick and raise the dead. And you've taught us the first two — and taught us well. What are we going to do about the next two?"

And he said, "Oh yes, I can see where that might be a problem for you. I think I will have to go out and find out how to do that."

So the next day he put in for his visa to the U.S.

Dr. Mikao Usui

Now in the middle-to-late 1800s this was very difficult to get. And so he had to wait many months. But the minute it came through, he resigned his post in the Christian School and came to the United States. Because, he thought, since Christianity came from the United States surely they will have the keys there —

So he went to the University of Chicago, and enrolled there in their theological seminary and attended for seven years until he got his Doctorate of Theology.

During the time he was there he was constantly writing to bishops of various sects and churches, asking them if their particular religion knew how to heal the sick; how to heal the body. And their answer was always "No, I'm sorry. We do not. We send sick people to doctors. We are busy healing the spirit."

This was the answer to every request he made — with a few exceptions. And when he checked them out, they didn't work.

During the years he had been studying theology, of course he had several courses in comparative religions. And because he had been raised a Christian, he was amazed to discover the Buddha!

He was as amazed as Christians here are to discover the Buddha, and to find here a man who had preceded Jesus by several hundred years and was purported to have done all the things that Jesus did: taught very similar lessons, bilocated, walked on water, healed the sick, raised the dead and all these same experiences.

4

And he thought, "Well, maybe the Buddhists kept their records. I guess I'll have to return home and check out the Buddhists."

Which he did.

At that time there were 16 or 17 Buddhist sects in Japan. So he started with the largest, which was in Tokyo.

He didn't just go to the head of each sect; he went to each temple in each sect — because they're completely autonomous. (It's not like they have a head hierarchy like the churches in the United States. Each temple there is completely autonomous.)

So he started with the largest and moved down with each of the sects. And he got the same answer always when he asked "Do you know how to heal the body?" The same thing the Christians told him: "No, we send sick people to the doctor. We're very busy healing the spirit."

And he traveled and traveled and traveled.

Finally he came to the very last monastery. And it was a little tiny one back in Kyoto. And when he asked to see the bishop of that monastery, this little tiny man about 72 years old with a little round baby face came forth.

When Dr. Usui asked if they knew how to heal the body — "Does the Zen know how to heal the body?" — he said "No longer."

And Usui said, "No *longer?*" You mean at one time this temple knew how to heal the body!"

And he said, "Oh yes. But we discovered that when we healed the body, the man was sick of spirit. He was not whole. So we spent so much time healing the spirit, we've forgotten how to heal the body. And we find that when we heal the spirit and don't heal the body, the man's not whole. But now we don't know how to heal the body anymore."

Mount Kurama-yama is just outside of Kyoto. It's a large holy mountain north of the city.

And Usui swung around and faced Mount Kurama-yama, and threw up his hands and said, "This is the end! *This* is the last place I had to search. All these years, and there's no place else to go! I'm through. I'm finished."

And the little monk said, "Usui sansei, forgive me for speaking. But I must tell you the Zen never say "This is the end." We always say "This is the beginning.' And we believe that when one door closes another one opens. And *I* believe that if you are truly dedicated and if you do not give up in your quest, you will again learn how to heal the body. Because if it was once known, it can be known again."

And Usui said, "You truly believe this?"

He said, "I do, or I would not say this to you."

And Usui said, "You're the only one who has ever given me any hope. May I study with you?"

He said, "Of course. All are welcomed by the Zen."

So Usui moved into that monastery and had a small cell there. And for three years, from early in the morning at first light until it was so dark you read no longer, he read the *sutras* in Japanese.

And he remembered what the little monk said: "He said if I don't find it I'm not going deep enough. And I'm determined I am going to find the answer! And all the great scholars study in Chinese. I will learn Chinese!"

And he did. He took his doctorate in Chinese ... until he could read and understand to perfection.

Again for three years, from first light until dark he read the *sutras* in Chinese — and found nothing.

And he thought, "I will not give up! I am not going deep enough. Buddhism came to us from India. I will learn Sanskrit."

And he did. He learned Sanskrit until he could read and understand to perfection. And he started to read the *sutras* in original Sanskrit.

And in that language he found the key. He found the key to healing the body.

Of course, he was ecstatic! He rushed to the bishop, a new bishop (since the little old bishop of years before had passed over). But the new bishop was as interested in what Dr. Usui was doing as the old bishop.

So Usui said to him, "Look!!! I have found the keys. I have found how to do this thing. They talk about the *power* —

"How am I going to gain the power?"

And the bishop said, "I think first we should meditate and pray." And Usui said, "I think so too."

So they both went to their cells after dinner that night, and each in his own way meditated and prayed on how Usui was to find the power.

They came together after breakfast the next morning. And it was decided that Usui should go out to Mount Kurama-yama to a specific level facing east, and for 21 days and nights he should fast and meditate. Hopefully then something would be shown to him —

So Usui got himself ready. And as he was leaving the compound that morning, there was a little 8-year-old boy from the monastery at the gate.

Usui looked down at that little fellow and said, "Son, I'm going out to Mount Kurama-yama and I'm going to fast and meditate for 21 days and nights. And I should be back here at twilight on the twenty-first day. But if I'm not, then you come out the morning of the twenty-second day and get my bones — because I'm dead."

And the little boy said, "Yes sir, Usui sansei! I will do that."

And Usui went the seventeen-and-a-half miles to his appointed place on Mount Kurama-yama. When he arrived there he realized he had no watch, no calendar. So he gathered up 21 small stones and piled them up in front of him. And each morning as he began his meditation, he'd pick up a stone and throw it away. And that's how he kept his calendar.

He later told Dr. Hyashi (whom he appointed head of the Masters when Usui made his transition), "You know, you have heard it said it is so dark before the dawn? It is true. It's so dark you cannot see your hand in front of your face. That is true. Because on the morning of the twenty-first day when I was finishing my meditation and I had finished my fast, I groped around until I had found the stone. I held it up and I could not even see it. And I held it there and I prayed. And I said, 'My Father, my God, this is the morning of the twenty-first day. I pray you will show me the light.' And I threw the stone away."

And in that way over on the horizon, as he did that, he saw a little bitty beam of light. And it started moving towards him. As it moved, it came faster and faster and got larger and larger and it frightened him nearly to death.

He jumped to his feet and turned to run, as he was really afraid! He thought to himself, "If that hits me, it'll kill me!"

Then he caught himself. And he swung around and shouted "*No!* I have spent years in my search. I have just asked to be shown the light. I will *not* run away!"

He placed his feet and braced himself, and said, "Father, if it kills me, I'll accept the light."

And he said that when he made that decision, this light simply burst upon him. It struck him in the middle of his forehead and knocked him to the ground, unconscious. And he told Hyashi that he believed that at that moment he died.

The next thing he knew, he saw bubbles … millions and millions of bubbles all moving from right to left in every color of the rainbow. From the palest pink to the deepest cerise; from the palest green to the deepest emerald; palest aqua to the deepest blue. And after all these gorgeous colors the gold came, and in the gold the white lights. And in the center of every white bubble was a gold figure in the Sanskrit that he had learned and read in the *sutras*.

And the bubble would come and stop, as though it would say "Here, Usui, learn this so you will know it always and be able to use it." And it would go. And then another would come and stop. And he was so afraid that he'd miss something that he told Hyashi he didn't even blink!

Finally he felt he had it all, and said, "Thank you, God. Now I have it. I know I can use it. Thank you, thank you, thank you."

And he said the next thing he knew, he opened his eyes and it was broad daylight! It was the middle of the morning.

And then he thought, "Ahhhhh! What a fantastic experience!"

He got to his feet, and he thought, "I'll go back down the mountain and tell the bishop about this wonderful thing. I hope I am strong enough."

And he started beating the dust off his shoes, flicked the pine needles and the dirt off his robe, put his hat on and grasped his staff … and thought "That's the *first* miracle! I've fasted for 21 days and nights and I'm *strong!* I can go all the way to Kyoto without any problem. It truly is a miracle."

He got so excited, he took off running down the

mountainside. And he stubbed his toe on a rock and tore his toenail clear back.

And he did what all of us would have done. He sat right down and grabbed it, and said *"Ohhh!"* He held it with both hands. And he thought, "Ah, that feels very strange. I'll keep holding it until it quits hurting." Which it did.

When he took his hands away it was completely healed. And he thought to himself, "Ah! That's the *second* miracle!"

So he progressed on down the mountainside. And he came to a bench with a red blanket on it with an ashtray in the middle. (And to this very day up in the mountains way back in Japan, that means fast-food service — a Japanese McDonalds.) So he thought he'd stop and have some breakfast. Which he did.

And while the man was preparing him breakfast, his little daughter came out of the little hutch that they lived in. She looked like a little cartoon character: she had this rag tied around her head, with this big knotty thing on top with one side of her face all pushed out. And she was crying and crying.

Usui said to her, "My dear child, what is the matter?"

And she said, "Oh good monk, I have this terrible toothache. And we live too far from Kyoto, I can't go there. We're too poor to pay a dentist. And it just hurts so bad!"

And he said, "Well, you come and sit here before me and let's see if I can help you."

So she did. She kneeled before him. And he put his hands upon her, putting one hand on the side of her swollen face.

And she said, "Oh sir, you are no ordinary monk."

And he said, "Why do you say that, child?"

She said, "Oh, your hands are so hot!" After a few more minutes she said, "Oh! You make magic. My tooth has stopped hurting!"

He said, "Isn't that wonderful. That's the *third* miracle."

So then he had his breakfast — and that was the *fourth* miracle. Because after fasting for 21 days he was able to eat all those wonderful things that the Japanese think make a fine breakfast … raw fish and pickled plums and all that wonderful stuff! Believe me, *that* was a miracle!

So he went down to Kyoto. And when he got to the door of the monastery and knocked on the door, the little boy came to the door and said, "Oh, Usui sansei! I'm so glad to see you! I had all my friends together and we were coming out first thing in the morning for your bones!"

Usui said, "Thank you very much. But as you can see, that won't be necessary now. Where is the bishop?"

The little boy said, "Oh, I have sad news, such sad sad news."

"What's the matter?"

He said, "The bishop is in his little cell with his feet on a hibachi, all wrapped up in a blanket because his arthritis is nearly killing him."

And Usui said, "Oh I'm sorry to hear that. I will have something to eat, then get a bath, and then I will go tell him about the wonderful things which have happened to me." Which he did.

And with the bishop's permission, he was sitting with one hand on his hip and one hand on his back where his arthritis grew. Meanwhile, he talked about this wonderful experience that he had had. And after he had been talking to the man for a few minutes, the bishop turned to Usui and said, "Usui, you made magic!"

Usui inquired, "What's happening?"

He said, "My arthritis has stopped hurting me!"

Usui said, "Isn't that wonderful. That is the Reiki. That's the Reiki that has been lost for so long! Now how am I best going to use it?"

And the bishop said, "Well, I think we should meditate and pray a lot." And Usui said, "Oh I agree."

So they each went to their own room and spent that night in meditation and prayer.

And they came together after breakfast the next morning, and was decided between them that Usui should go down to Beggar City and heal the beggars so they could go get new names at the temple and become responsible citizens, having jobs for themselves and supporting their families.

(And that was wonderful. Except that I don't know what you know about the beggar culture in the Orient. To this very day, the Beggar King is like 20 notches above the Godfather in the United States, okay?

I mean absolutely nothing nefarious goes on in any department that the Beggar King does not control completely and thoroughly — including life and death.)

So Usui thought, "That is a wonderful idea. But how am I going to get down there and get accepted?"

Well, he decided the thing to do was to dress up like a beggar (you know, like a peddler). Which he did. He got himself a little cart and stacked some vegetables on it, put on some clothes like a peddler's, and started down the street.

Well, within a block he found himself a couple of beggars. No problem there! And he went up to them and said, "I want you to take me to your king."

"Oh no!"

He said, "I have a wonderful gift for him."

"Let's see it!"

He said, "I cannot show it to you. I can only give it to him."

"You can't show it to us?"

"No. I can only give it to him."

They said, "Do you know what kind of position you have put us in? If what you have for him he doesn't like, and we take you there, he'll kill us. All three of us! And if we tell you no, and he finds out about it and he wanted it, he'll kill us. So no matter what we do, we are in trouble. How come you asked us to do this thing?"

Usui told them, "Because I have this wonderful thing, and this is what I need to do."

Well, they took him. And when they arrived he had to explain to the Beggar King what this wonderful thing was: he wanted to come down and work among his people, and heal them so they could go and have whole, new lives.

And the Beggar King said, "That is the *dumbest* thing I ever heard in my life! Once a beggar, always a beggar."

And Usui said, "I don't believe that. I believe they can really have new lives."

And the Beggar King said, "It's not going to cost me anything, so I don't care if you try. But first we have to have the initiation if you want to work down here."

And Usui said, "I don't care. What?"

And he said, "First, take the fruit and vegetables, sell the cart and put the money in my coffers." Which Usui did. "Now your clothing is far too fine for you to be working down here among the beggars. So take his clothing. Take his clothes!" They stripped him. "Sell the clothes. Put the money in my coffers."

And of course when they stripped Usui they found his moneybelt. The Beggar King said, "A belt full of gold, and you're going to work among beggars? Never! Put it in my coffers." Which they did.

And Usui said, "I can't work like *this,* stark naked." So they threw him some old vermin-infested rags, saying "There you are. Clothes. First-class beggar clothes. Put them on." Which he did.

Then Usui spoke. "There has to be one agreement. I'm going to be working healing from morning to night. And you will have to feed me. I will have no time to search for food. You will have to see that I'm fed."

The Beggar King said, "Humgh! Well, we pick up garbage. And what we don't eat, we will throw to you."

Usui agreed. "That's all right. But you will have to feed me."

So for seven years Usui worked with the beggars. He healed everything that came to him. He started with the young people, the children. (Because as I told you, the shorter the condition has been in effect, the faster it heals.)

As soon as he healed them, they went to the temple where the priests gave them new names.

Usui had worked himself out of work after seven years, and he had time to take little evening constitutionals.

And as he was walking around Beggar City among all these funny looking tin huts and cardboard glued together, he kept seeing faces that looked very familiar to him. And one evening he walked up to a young man and said, "Will you please tell me why you look so familiar to me?"

And the young man said, "Ah, Dr. Usui. You know me. Of course you know me. I'm one of the first fellows that you healed down here!"

Usui exclaimed, "I healed you? *I healed you?* If I healed you, what are you doing here? I sent you out to make a new name, to make a new life!"

And he said, "Oh I did that."

"You did that?"

He said, "Sure. But do you know how much self-discipline it takes to get up and go to work every day? Do you know how hard I had to work for just a few pennies? And we were *still* hungry all the time. I would rather be a beggar!"

And Usui sank to his knees. "What, oh what have I done? The churches were right. A person has to be healed of spirit as well as of body. Reiki given away makes beggars of people!"

And he dropped to the ground and just rubbed his head into the dirt.

Then he stood up and said, "I cut off all beggars. Never again will Reiki be given away. Always the flow will have to be completed. Always there will have to be an exchange with Reiki. And now I know how to heal the body *and* the spirit — "

And he knocked the dirt of Beggar City off his feet, and went back up to Kyoto.

What Dr. Usui had discovered was the Five Principles of Reiki.

- ◆ ONE: *"Today I give thanks for my many blessings."*
- ◆ TWO: *"Just for today I will not worry."*
- ◆ THREE: *"Today I will not be angry."*
- ◆ FOUR: *"Today I will do my work honestly."*
- ◆ FIVE: *"Today I will be kind to my neighbor and to every living thing."*

And we believe that if you bring these principles into your life and give yourself a Reiki treatment every day, then you will have health, happiness, prosperity and a long life.

So when Usui got back to Kyoto, he got himself bathed and in some decent clothing, and he found the biggest torch he could find. A huge torch.

And the next morning, bright sunshiny morning, at 10 o'clock he lit this torch and stood on the busiest corner in Kyoto. And everybody that walked by, "Ha, ha, ha, ha!" They thought he was crazy.

Finally a young fellow walked up to him and said, "Sir, will you please tell me why you feel you need a light at 10 o'clock on a bright sunshiny morning? Standing here on a street corner?"

And Usui said, "You see that torch? That is because I am hunting for people who do not want illness in a home, who do not want to have a lot of big doctors' bills, who want to learn how to live in a good fun-fulfilled life. And if you want to know the story of Reiki, you come to that temple over there at 7 o'clock tonight and you can bring all of that into your life."

And that was the beginning of Usui's traveling teaching. He went from Hokkaido in the north to the very southern-most province. On his travels he acquired 18 disciples, young men who traveled with him.

When it came time for Usui to make his transition, he had two children but they did not want to dedicate their lives to Reiki. So he chose Dr. Chugiro Hyashi, who had been one of his disciples.

And when Hyashi decided he wanted to make his transition — this was before the Second World War, because he felt he was dedicated to healing and not to killing. He had two children (a son and a daughter). They did not want to dedicate their lives to Reiki, so he chose my master, Hawayo Takata.

Takata was the first woman and the first American, the first person not of the elite section of Japan to have Reiki. She died last December [1980]. And since Usui's day, each master has taken steps that Reiki will never be lost again ... so that Reiki will never die.

And that's the Reiki story.

"Miracles are only things that happen under laws we don't yet understand."

— Virginia Samdahl

2
Philosophy and Procedures

Reiki is a Japanese word which means "Universal Life Energy."

Everyone is born with Reiki. It is the energy of life itself. It is the energy that emanates from the hands of a Reiki therapist.

In the words of Master Nonie C. Greene, the embodiment of Reiki can be described as "a 'tap in' with the cosmic, universal force." It is, she continues, the "white-light energy which is a transforming energy on all levels of a person's beingness. ... Reiki is a universal truth. It is simple and direct, can be done at any time or place, requires no equipment, and literally the 'essence' of the Reiki classes — that is, the transmissions and the hand positions — could be taught to any and all intellects and nationalities with little translating."

This workbook is based on Usui Shiko Ryoho, meaning "The Usui System of Natural Healing" and named after Dr. Mikao Usui who rediscovered the system when studying the sacred *sutras* in the late 1800s.

The Usui System is a healing art that utilizes this universal life energy power, by channeling it through our bodies for storage in the solar plexus and into the dis-eased individual for rebalancing through "laying on of hands." The System is available to all who seek freedom from pain and suffering.

What makes Reiki different from other forms of natural healing?

Reiki can not be taught as ordinary knowledge is. Instead, it is transmitted by the meditation and touch of a Reiki master to a student. Then its application is explained through demonstration and information, such as your instructor and this workbook provide.

And it can be used by nearly anyone, even young children.

"In most forms of spiritual and psychic healing, you have to *work!*" exclaims Reiki Master Virginia W. Samdahl. "There's this big thing about altering consciousness, getting centered in your head at 10.5 cycles per second, and learning to hold that while healing then takes place.

"And once I started using Reiki, none of this was true. It was *so easy* and *so simple*. And these miraculous things happened over and over.

"And my head wasn't ready for this," Mrs. Samdahl confides, "and I don't know if yours is. I kept asking, 'What happened to this idea that I'm just-a-channel? Because how can I be a channel when I'm not doing anything to *be* a channel?'

"So I did a lot of meditating. And it came to me that we are *more* than a channel," she continues, referring to the student once he (she) receives the power transfers. "We *are* Reiki. We *are* universal life energy. We're *more* than just a conduit, a sewer that the stuff runs through.

"It's the God within us that does the powerful works. Not the ego I am, but the God I Am; the Reiki, the universal life energy. And that's what we are made of. So without us the healing could not take place.

"So you're more than a channel. You're a channel, yes, but you are more than that.

"So remember: *Without you the healing could not take place*. You have to love, love enough and care enough to reach out and touch — to place your hands on another — to make anything happen."

And happen things will!

Reiki Master Barbara St. John shared the following story in *The Reiki Review* [II-1]:

A long story short, I spilled scalding hot coffee down the insides of both legs as I was driving in a car. Needless to say, I was in excruciating pain. All I knew to do was Reiki. Alas, my hands weren't large enough to cover the area simultaneously. But the Reiki took the entire pain away within twenty minutes and I was able to continue to a wholistic doctor who diagnosed the burns as second-degree, told me to do Reiki, and sent me away. Would you believe it never scabbed or blistered and was totally healed in less than two weeks…and there are no scars. That's incredible."

A less traumatic but no less revealing example (though in a much different way) is recalled by Reiki Master Samdahl:

I knew a young couple, and he was completely bald at age 32. He reduced his red meat intake, ate spirulina to keep his protein up and used vitamin E oil on his scalp, as prescribed by Reiki. And after they'd get the dishes out of the way in the evening he would sit down in front of her while they watched television, and she'd treat the back of his head and he'd treat the front of his head. And within a year he had a full head of hair!

While baldness in the third decade of life is somewhat unusual (not to mention such a dramatic rejuvenation of the scalp's follicles), accidental scrapes and cuts to the very young are commonplace. Fortunately age is no obstacle to Reiki:

> Brandon, at the age of 12 months, fell on a graveled driveway and cut his mouth badly. It was streaming blood. His father, a Reiki therapist, grabbed him up into his arms and put his hand over his son's mouth. After about 15 seconds the baby pulled his face away from his father's hand and there was no vestige of injury.

Your instructor and probably classmates as well will have many anecdotes to relate, which you might like to note at the end of this section.

THE REIKI ETHIC

"One of the reasons we're so concerned about healing in our culture is because we differentiate it from other kinds of God's work. How come it's okay to be a masseuse, a mechanic, a therapist, but not a healer?"

asks Mrs. Samdahl. "That's really dumb!

"Over the centuries we have separated spirit, mind, and body. We've made ourselves a triumvirate instead of a one. And now we have done the same thing with the healing ethic. And it's high time we get it back together where it belongs — that we are just portions of God's essence serving Him the best way we know how..."

For yourself, that service will probably now include Reiki.

What are some of the unique features that comprise the Reiki ethic?

- ◆ Reiki brings the body into harmony by relieving physical and emotional blockages.

- ◆ Reiki heals the cause and eliminates the effects of an imbalance.

- ◆ Reiki helps minimize your sense of helplessness when facing disease or the trauma of modern society.

- ◆ Reiki can be used in conjunction with standard medical procedures and religious beliefs without conflict.

- ◆ Reiki helps lower the increasing cost of conventional medical care, easing strain on your budget.

- ◆ Reiki is completely impersonal. "That is," as Mrs. Samdahl says, "you can't mess up! You don't get the human feeling in there."

♦ _____
_____
_____
_____

♦ _____
_____
_____

♦ _____
_____

♦ _____
_____

"One of the basic concepts of the wholistic approach to life and living is to assume *responsibility* for your health and well-being," points out Reiki Master Barbara D. Weber Ray. Thus Reiki is particularly advantageous, she says, because it "is a technique which allows you to assume this responsibility naturally."

Reiki is a method based also on intent. You must be conscious when administering a treatment. But the client may go into sleep level. You can talk during treatment, which is for many an additional form of therapy (psychological and emotional).

"In all my years of experience in the healing arts," says Dr. Weber, "I have never encountered a natural healing system as complete and as effective as Reiki. It is indeed an honor to be able to teach Reiki to others so that

we may all achieve our Divine birthright: wellness and wholeness."

REIKI CERTIFICATION

Certification in (Usui) Reiki is divided into these three degrees:

♦ *First-degree* training traditionally consists of four sessions of approximately 2½ hours each, in which a 20% power transfer is administered by the teacher and finally sealed in the student.

The basic Reiki principles and methods for treating various ailments in oneself and others are taught.

♦ *Second-degree* consists of full 100% power transfer, and traditionally is not administered until at least 90 days after first-degree certification so the Reiki can be worked with and integrated within the student.

It allows you to accelerate the treatment time; deal with mental and emotional problems of a client; and apply a unique method of absent healing.

♦ *Third-degree* is that of the master, and means the person can teach Reiki and confer first- and second-degree through power transfers.

It can be conferred only by an individual who has received the special Reiki keys rediscovered by Dr. Usui — to a person who is totally dedicated and committed to teaching Natural Healing as exemplified by the Usui Ryoho System.

This workbook is designed for the first-degree student in accordance with the format of Reiki instruction used by Grand Master Hawayo Takata, who received her training directly from Dr. Hyashi, the grand master taught by Dr. Usui himself.

The desire to learn and the initiations are all you need to heal in the Usui system.

Once initiated into first-degree, anyone can heal.

It does not require special talent, nor can it be done wrongly.

The more the therapist uses Reiki, the stronger it becomes.

Reiki will never leave once sealed in the student, except if he attempts to misrepresent the process by claiming to teach and give power transfers without the knowledge that comes with third-degree certification.

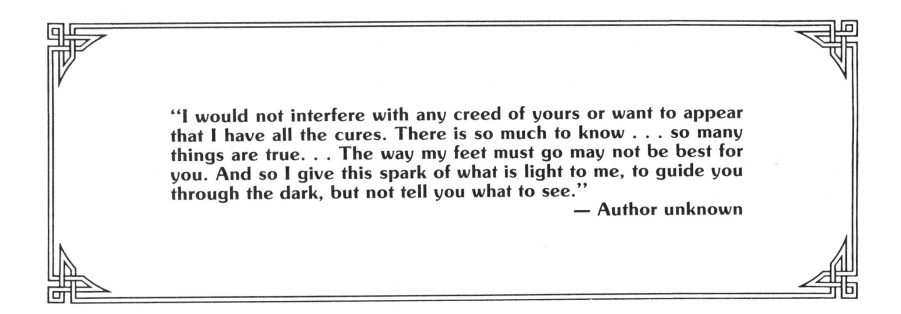

"I would not interfere with any creed of yours or want to appear that I have all the cures. There is so much to know . . . so many things are true. . . The way my feet must go may not be best for you. And so I give this spark of what is light to me, to guide you through the dark, but not tell you what to see."

— Author unknown

REIKI PRINCIPLES

Five basic principles form the Tao — the attitude towards self and life — for the Reiki therapist. They are calligraphied (and suitable for framing) at the end of this chapter.

Meditate on the meaning of these principles. Share and discuss your insights with others. Reflect also on the "Reiki Affirmation" (Chapter 11), phrased by Virginia Samdahl to succinctly define what Reiki is.

Other basic rules to know about Reiki include these precepts:

"Reiki is simple. Reiki is doing what's natural!"

"Hands on, Reiki turns on. Hands off, Reiki turns off."
The life force makes no mistakes, and the power transfers given by a Reiki master last your entire life.

"Always use Reiki with common sense."

"You have to realize that most of us are as well as we want to be."

"You pick up nothing from the client. Everything goes from you to them.
Therefore, you do not pick up their complaint."

"Never, never diagnose or prescribe. Simply state what you would do if *you* had the condition perceived."

"To give Reiki away makes beggars of people."

"You don't have to treat everyone, and you don't have to feel guilty about it."

"You are Reiki. God is the source. You are hooked into God. You are a divine being. Reiki is divine."

"Once opened, there's no way to shut Reiki off. And why would you? It is healing, an expression of love."

WHO TO TREAT

First, treat yourself. You are Reiki and can be in as perfect of health as your ego will allow yourself to express.

Next, treat family members. Normally the family unit will have provided you with many benefits, and transmitting the health of Reiki is an excellent way to complete the exchange.

Third, consider treating anyone who asks. Asking is important. Because Reiki is a system based on *intent*, the prospective client should express his intent for health by requesting the treatment.

(Refer to Chapter 12 for insight into intent and subconscious agreement between client and healer.)

Naturally if the person is in coma, or an infant, or someone whose family asks for the healing, or someone for who you are responsible, it is appropriate to do Reiki.

By stating in your mind, "You are free to accept or reject this healing as you will," you release the will of the client and do not impose your will upon them.

Be cautious in treating an accident victim you don't know, in that it is legally advisable not to say anything about your healing ability.

Simply attempt to administer Reiki in an inconspicuous manner — which fortunately is very easy with Reiki.

Speaking of infants, don't think babies — even fetuses — are too young to receive treatments.

"Reiki just works zing-o on babies," affirms Mrs. Samdahl enthusiastically. "They have no barriers whatsoever. They are *wide* open to God's love. And that's what healing is: God loving us."

Persons hospitalized or under conventional medical care can also be treated with Reiki.

If the patient takes medication, instruct him to regularly consult with his physician — because as Reiki rebalances his body the prescribed dosage might have to be lessened to avoid overdose.

Do not diagnose illnesses and prescribe medicines, however, unless you are an M.D. Suggest, rather than direct: simply state what you'd do if *you* had the condition perceived, giving the patient the responsibility to assess its merits for himself.

It is also important to remember that you should *never* feel forced or obligated to heal someone, or guilty for not taking the time to heal whenever and wherever requested.

Don't forget pets, animals and plants, either. They have universal life energy, and Reiki works for them too.

"The *big bonus* with Reiki is that when you are treating someone else you are receiving a healing at the same time," says Mrs. Samdahl.

"One is never tired nor depleted after giving a treatment since we are using universal life energy, not our own."

While healing is generally thought of in terms of living creatures, this universal life energy pervades all creation.

Therefore, you can consider applying Reiki in some rather unorthodox healing situations. "WHAT" to treat can become as vital a consideration as "WHO" to treat.

Here are three interesting examples described in *The Reiki Review* [II-2]:

♦ A second-degree Reiki therapist used her hands (along with the absentee healing technique) to create a "love-meld" in a contentious parent-child conference. By placing a Reiki hand over the heart of each person during the conference, attitudes "changed immediately and the people were able to get beyond themselves and express concern and love."

♦ A plumber, certified as second-degree Reiki, discovered a dishwasher had been improperly wired. He stated the intent that his hands would 'heal' the appliance until a serviceman came, "and to even his amazement the wires did not burn up and it continued to work until it could be rewired."

♦ Reiki practitioners Sara Schmidlin and Mary Ann Fuller report "using the Reiki to nurse their cars around town and to keep the batteries running."

What unconventional uses for Reiki — as a constructive influence for the channeling of universal life energy — can you think of?

The possibilities can be as imaginative as creation is varied, and as workable too.

Discuss and list your ideas here:

_____

_____

_____

_____

_____

_____

_____

_____

_____

_____

COMPLETING THE FLOW OF EXCHANGE

As you know, one emphasized premise of Reiki is that it's not to be given away free.

This principle often distresses people, as your instructor will most surely point out. After all, say many, shouldn't healing — and natural healing specifically, such as Reiki — be viewed as a service freely given without charge to one's fellowman?

Rev. Carol Parrish-Harra — nationally recognized leader in the esoteric field and founder of two spiritual communities (Villa Serena, and Sparrow Hawk Village) — was taught what she called "an important aspect of spiritual law" by her first enlightened teacher:

> *… there must be an exchange of energy to keep the harmony of the universe.* We must receive to be able to give.
>
> If the river does not receive, it runs dry. If one does not receive, one breaks the flow just as if one refuses to give.
>
> In ancient times spiritual headers, teachers and seers received housing, food, clothing and gifts in exchange for their spiritual services. It has always been an accepted custom that they were supported by the people they served. In fact, it was considered a blessing to have a spiritually attuned one in residence in the area.
>
> In modern times money has become a commodity of exchange. Of course, we could and may return to a bartering system. Many people work out an exchange of goods for classes or treatments, and that is an excellent way. But, it usually is easiest for most people in our time and in our society to exchange money.
>
> It is important to emphasize that *money is merely energy in an easily exchanged method.* Five dollars may be paid for an hour of someone's labor or two hours of another's … the money represents mental and/or physical effort, the energy they expended…
>
> This exchange generally frees them of other concerns so they can concentrate on being a capable channel being free to respond to the needs of those who are inclined to seek them out.
>
> Remember also, in this exchange of energy (represented by money or other forms), we free ourselves of obligation when receiving their services.
>
> Of course, a fairness is required on the part of both; and discrimination. Keeping a balance in relationships is what makes them healthy and happy experiences for us.*

---

* Carol Parrish-Harra: "To Charge or Not To Charge," *Rainbows* (LIFE SPECTRUMS, Harrisburg, PA 17108-0373), II-1, 2-3.

How does this "spiritual law" integrate with the Reiki philosophy and healer?

"The healer who will accept nothing is egotistical," answers Mrs. Samdahl. "They're putting themselves in a position where they will not let a person pay his human obligations. They are keeping that person indebted, not only in this lifetime but into eternity.

"Always remember, the Tao must complete itself. If everything comes in and doesn't go out, you become like the Dead Sea and die. If everything goes out, you dry up and become like a mud bed. If there is a balanced in-and-out flow, you are like a beautiful lake — everything in and around it grows and blossoms."

And what of the argument that Jesus the Nazarene never charged for His healing?

Consider this viewpoint, as expressed by Reiki Master Samdahl:

"When you're told 'Jesus never charged for healing,' ask 'How do you know? Were you there?' He ran around with his whole gang of guys, and everyone of them had left their visible means of support. Right? Everyone of 'em had walked off the job! They all had good clothes … they all had good sandals … they all had plenty to eat and someplace to sleep … and they had Judas Iscariot as treasurer to keep their money. Where was it coming from? Somebody was paying for something.

"So you are *worth your time*. And that's all you're getting paid for — your time. *And you are worth your time*."

So give the Reiki client the opportunity to pay his way, thereby freeing him of the burden of obligation to you.

But that value on your time need not be reimbursed by money paid directly into your pocket.

You can maintain the flow of exchange immediately by making a donation on your behalf to a church or favored charity, for example.

Barter is another way. Linda Bush, a classmate of the authors, told the story of a young girl in a dining room who got chlorine in her eyes. She asked for a Reiki treatment immediately, which was cheerfully exchanged for a bite of the young girl's chocolate pudding.

Your instructor will likely wish to share additional insights on this point, and you'll want to record them along with more ways to complete "the flow of exchange" in Reiki here:

_____

_____

_____

_____

_____

_____

_____

HOW TO TREAT

Your Reiki master will cover this topic in great detail, because this is the very core of Reiki.

As a prelude to that instruction, here are some basic points to know:

♦ First, create an environment as quiet, comfortable and soothing as possible for treatment.

In the home, set aside a room or designate a small area to be regularly used for client treatment. This "Reiki space" will become familiar (and thus psychologically comfortable) for clients that require successive treatments and also becomes charged with the nature of Reiki itself, thereby facilitating the healing experience.

♦ Wear comfortable clothing that won't interfere with the treatment positions.

For male patients: remove their glasses, vest, jacket, tie and belt, shoes; have his pockets emptied.

For female patients: remove their glasses, shoes, belt, scarves, and jewelry around the neck; no girdles or tight pantyhose.

No terribly snug pants in either case.

♦ Most treatments by first-degree practitioners are hands-on. Remote, or absentee healing is taught in second-degree Reiki.

However, occasionally it may not be possible to possible to touch the patient directly due to severe skin lesions or second/third-degree burns, or thick layers of clothing, or a plaster cast. Or you may wish to treat an infant and don't want to disturb his shallow sleep.

Know that Reiki remains effective even when your hands are an inch over the body's surface.

The Reiki Finish does require direct physical contact with the skin, though.

♦ Maintain proper hygiene for yourself, just as you would expect from any medical professional.

Always have clean hands, washing with soap before treatment and afterwards for 20-30 seconds in cool running water to break the energy flow. If in an emergency situation water is not available, form the hands in the "prayer" position with fingertips together and press firmly for 30 seconds.

♦ Place a box of kleenex tissues, plus a blanket or sheet, within easy reach.

The tissues are for eye treatment and certain ailments; the covers, for the client's comfort.

♦ Have the client lie down, if possible, so gravity can aid in pulling Reiki into his body.

Place a pillow under his head; another under his knees to relieve pressure on the lower back. Employ the sheet or light blanket if the client complains of chills.

Don't neglect to ensure your own needs, either.

Remember: *The comfort of yourself and the client is the next most important thing to Reiki itself during a treatment.*

♦ Make sure the client's feet are not crossed. This tends to 'short circuit' the energy flow.

♦ Tell the client he may feel worse after the first or second treatment, either due to severe imbalance in an organ (or the body generally) or because you may stop treatment just as the illness has been brought back from the chronic state to its acute stage before eventual release.

If this happens, a minimum of three — preferably four — consecutive daily treatments will be required unless healing takes place after the first or second treatment.

"The disease must return from where it came," is a basic Reiki tenet.

♦ Ask the client about ailments irritated by touching. Also inquire about any major surgery.

♦ "Notify people what you're going to do," says Mrs. Samdahl with a grin, "so you don't scare them to death."

♦ *"Treat HEAD, FRONT and BACK, and hold anything that hurts — and you can't go wrong!"*

That, according to Reiki masters, is the basic rule of Reiki treatment. Think of the front (neck to waist) as the "Master Motor" of the body.

♦ Keep your fingers together; otherwise, energy is scattered. Rather than making them stiff and flat, curve the fingers just slightly so they rest easily upon the contours of the body.

Imagine you are going to touch your lover in a gentle embrace, and you'll get it just perfect!

♦ Begin by spending 8-to-10 minutes on each Reiki position.

As you practice Reiki and your biosensory system becomes more acute to the universal life energy, you will sense a varying rhythmic rise-and-fall of energy under your hands. Your power to channel Reiki will also increase, and treatment time will shorten.

Extremely diseased centers will probably need prolonged treatments, just as with conventional medicine.

Whatever, your hands will tell you through this sinusoidal pattern when to break: Do so at the end of the first cycle of peak-to-ebb flow, just as the energy is about to rise again. That completes one energy cycle for that particular organ of the body drawing in the most Reiki.

Each period will differ, depending on the organ and its condition.

♦ If the client has organs missing due to surgery, treat as if they are present anyway.

Reiki can help set up an energy pattern within the body to balance the body as if that organ were physically present, and will release adhesions if they exist.

♦ A *cold spot* indicates a dysfunctioning organ or impaired circulation. Hold the area until it feels warm to your touch.

♦ "There is no such thing as a *partial* treatment — because the body is *all linked in*, as you know!

"For instance," explains Mrs. Samdahl, "if a person has diabetic blindness, you are not going to cure the eyes [placement HEAD # 1] until you cure the pancreas [FRONT # 2] — because the pancreas is what manufactures insulin and a lack of insulin is what creates diabetes and diabetes is what can create diabetic blindness, et cetera. So until the pancreas is healed, nothing is going to happen to diabetic blindness."

So aside from emergency situations, always give the Whole Body treatment before focusing on particular ailments for additional Reiki. As you are giving of your time, the client should be equally agreeable to give of his time for a proper treatment. The client has given you the authority by requesting a Reiki treatment, so be firm about what you know must be done.

If *partial treatment* must be done, treat the solar plexus and adrenals. (This is also good for energy revitalization and "bringing things back to life.")

♦ Reiki is pulled through the body at a rate corresponding to the need of the client.

The more energy needed to regenerate, rejuvenate and revitalize the injured body, the longer the healing will generally take.

"At the end of 10 minutes almost every organ has all the Reiki it needs," is Mrs. Samdahl's guideline.

♦ **TEAM TREATMENTS.** When possible, pair up on FRONT and BACK positions. Treat FRONT # 1 and # 2 simultaneously.

Additionally, treatment on the torso and head is very beneficial.

Also when possible, have one healer hold the soles of the client's feet as a means to boost his energy field.

♦ **REIKI FINISH.** When the client has accepted all the Reiki needed at one session, conclude his treatment with the Reiki Finish — it's like "icing on the cake."

a) Have the client lie on his stomach and bare his back, pushing aside the shirt or blouse to the shoulders and unhooking a lady's bra straps.

b) Maintain hands-on contact once you begin.

c) Bend the client's left leg at the knee. Hold his foot and rotate the toes clockwise, then counterclockwise. Bend the toes up and down a few times. Vertically pivot his foot several times. Massage firmly his entire foot from toes to heel. Pinch the Achilles tendon (upper heel) 2 to 3 times. Grasp his leg above the ankle and shake the foot vigorously, then lay it down gently.

d) Stroke each leg gently but firmly from its ankle to the knee, then from the knee to the crotch. (Don't press on the back of the knee, as it is very sensitive.)

e) Repeat steps "c" and "d" for the right foot.

f) Standing alongside the client, reach across his body and knead his side between the hip and armpit with both hands using a push-pull motion "as if you were wringing out a wet rag." Then stroke up and down his side a few times, causing the skin to glow pink.

g) Keeping one hand on the client's body, move to

the client's other side and repeat step "f".

h) Knead the shoulder muscles and the base of the neck about 5 times.

i) With the flat edge of the thumbs, "scrub" up the channels on each side of the spine with short alternating advances going from the base of the spine to the neck.

j) *If the client has no diabetic tendency,* form a "V" with two fingers and place them at the base of the neck; place the other hand on top of the fingers' knuckles, and pull down along the channels flanking the spine.

For pancreatic conditions, use the above "up" motion stroke *only* from the base of the spine to the base of the neck — "for this cleanses the blood."

k) Make a pyramid with your hands, and place on buttocks and push up the spine and then out over the shoulders and draw down along his sides without lifting your hands. Repeat until the skin glows pink, indicating increased circulation.

l) Assist the client to sit up by asking him to grasp your arm above the elbow as you take his. Slide your other hand under his neck so as to support his head with your hand, and pull up as he raises himself. Make sure he isn't dizzy and can support himself, then release your grip and ask him to sit quietly one-to-two minutes before getting off the table and dressing.

♦ Wash your hands again, or press your fingertips together for 30 seconds to close down the energy flow.

The Reiki treatment is now complete … yet the effect of the Reiki on the cells and energy flow of the body does not end with the treatment, but continues to build and balance the cells and system.

EMOTIONAL/PSYCHOLOGICAL TRAUMA

Edgar Cayce claimed through broader consciousness that "mind is the builder." And metaphysicians have long taught that one's physical condition is a reflection of one's inner mental and emotional states.

Emotional and psychological blockages are among the most difficult to tap but, once released, most often the client's physical recovery is marvelously rapid.

Mrs. Samdahl affirms that a Reiki treatment "is a method of healing whereby the emotions and the body are brought into balance through the use of Universal Life Energy. The energy seems to direct itself to the problem without using the mind of the healer; the energy is self-directing."

Thus it is not unusual that a client, his emotional blockages released by Reiki, may find himself unexpectedly crying and becoming embarrassed because he came for "a physical healing" only.

Assure him this is a natural occurrence — a *vital* one — en route to whole-person cleansing and rebalance, and ease his apprehensions. And hand him a kleenex …

ON BEING CERTIFIED

Now that you are Reiki, realize anytime you touch someone or something the universal life energy turns on. Your Reiki is *the Midas touch* of healing.

Yet don't be disillusioned if forever after your first-degree certification you occasionally experience a physical or emotional distress. Reiki is not Nirvana or Heaven or omnipresent Bliss — though compared to what some people have chosen to suffer and how segments of the medical community treat (or can't treat) certain ailments, it may seem that way to the healed client.

Dis-ease and subsequent ailments will remain an aspect of mass consciousness for some time to come in this world's reality. So when you find yourself in a lowered energy state, remember Reiki works on you too!

And don't hesitate to request the aid of other Reiki therapists to magnify the universal life energy flow in you. Remember it was the Nazarene who said: "Where two or three are gathered ..."

The increase of universal life energy through Reiki affects more than your physical and emotional health, though.

"Reiki is an impetus to spiritual growth," says Reiki Master Phyllis Furumoto-Hartley. "Follow the happenings of life, they will lead you to places and people that will promote inner growth. Focal points or priorities of living will be altered. More and more you will find a quiet honesty about your actions and your lifestyle. Be prepared for growth and spiritual healing."

So use your Reiki hands ... in mixing foods, vitalizing water, and healing in *all* its myriad forms.

Your touch will feel good to others, too. Go hug lots of people!

Be prepared to experience growth, consciousness expansion, and spiritual strength.

And Reiki, Reiki, Reiki —

"The first wealth is health."
— Ralph Waldo Emerson,
The Conduct of Life

Notes: _____

_____

_____

_____

_____

_____

_____

_____

_____

_____

_____

_____

The Reiki Principles

Just for today I will give thanks for my many blessings.

Just for today I will not worry.

Just for today I will not be angry.

Just for today I will do my work honestly.

Just for today I will be kind to my neighbor and every living thing.

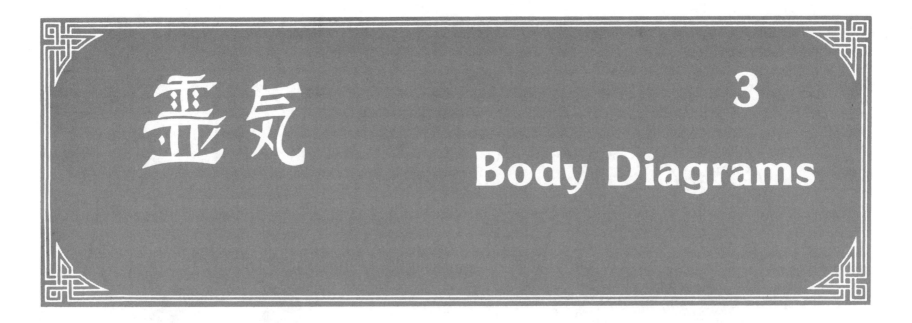

3
Body Diagrams

The following generalized diagrams of the human anatomy are not intended to be used for medical reference, rather as a practical guide to the physical location of a specific organ and its positioning in relationship to the other organs of the body. They are not complete as shown, but do contain the body's main internal physiological construction in a general view.

You may later find it necessary to refer to a more complete illustrated source. We can recommend the "Atlas of Human Anatomy" by the American Map Company (1926 Broadway, New York, NY 10023-6915); *Gray's Anatomy* (The Running Press, 38 S 19th Street, Philadelphia, PA 19103-3502); and *The Merck Manual* (Merck, Sharp & Dohme Research Laboratories, Merck & Company, Rahway, NJ 07065).

ENDOCRINE GLANDS:

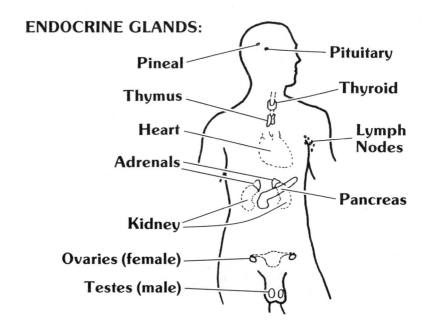

Pineal — Pituitary
Thymus — Thyroid
Heart — Lymph Nodes
Adrenals
Pancreas
Kidney
Ovaries (female)
Testes (male)

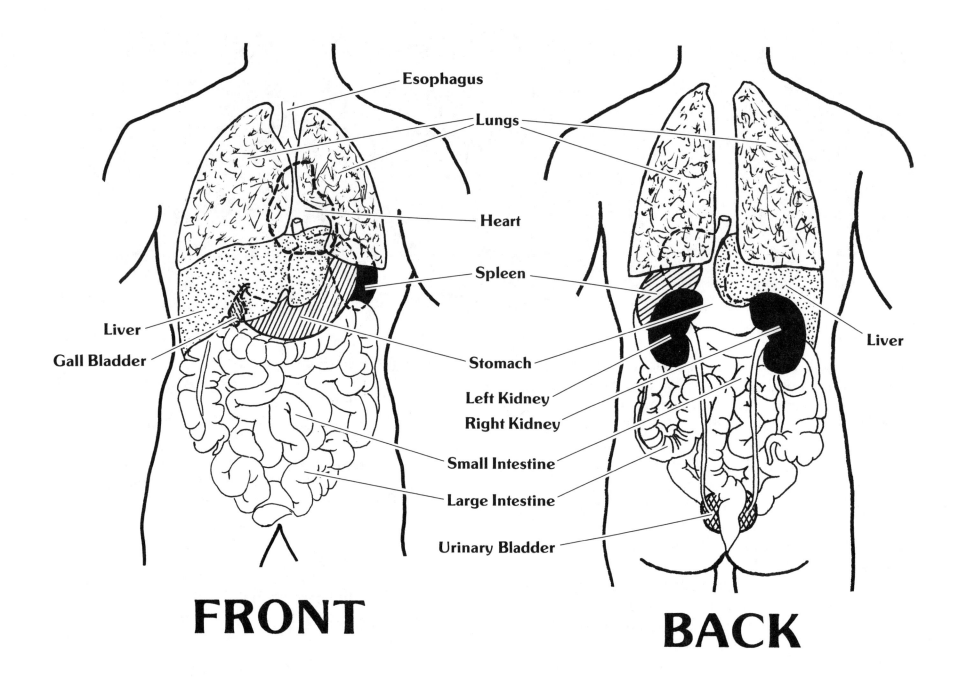

Esophagus

Lungs

Heart

Spleen

Liver

Gall Bladder

Liver

Stomach

Left Kidney

Right Kidney

Small Intestine

Large Intestine

Urinary Bladder

FRONT

BACK

32

4
Atlas of
Treatment Placements

This pictorial atlas catalogues the fourteen Reiki hand treatments placements that are basic to first-degree certification, and used in treating yourself and others. It is your key to using "the gentle loving hands of Reiki."

Your instructor will describe how, for reference points, you should visualize the body divided into four quadrants formed by a plane through the waist and another perpendicular to it along the center axis from the neck to the crotch.

Administering all placements to yourself or another constitutes a Whole Body treatment. Each placement in a regular health maintenance program should be held until the rise-and-fall of Reiki completes one cycle. Additional treatment for specific imbalances can then be given as described in the Glossary.

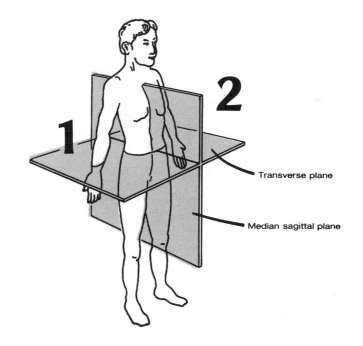

Transverse plane

Median sagittal plane

HEAD 1: (Self)

_____

_____

_____

_____

Notes: _____

_____

_____

_____

_____

_____

_____

_____

PSI PRESS

HEAD 2: (Self)

_____

_____

_____

_____

Notes: _____

_____

_____

_____

_____

_____

_____

_____

HEAD 3: (Self)

_____

_____

_____

_____

Notes: _____

_____

_____

_____

_____

_____

_____

_____

_____

HEAD 4: (Self)

_____

_____

_____

_____

Notes: _____

_____

_____

_____

_____

_____

_____

_____

PSI PRESS

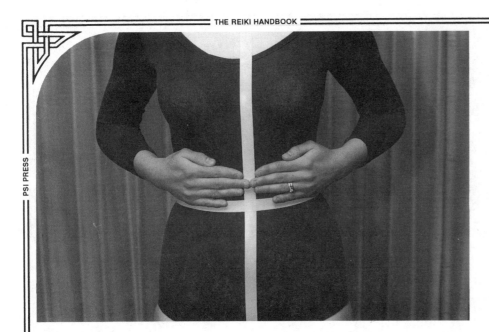

FRONT 1: (Self)

_____

_____

_____

_____

Notes: _____

_____

_____

_____

_____

_____

_____

_____

_____

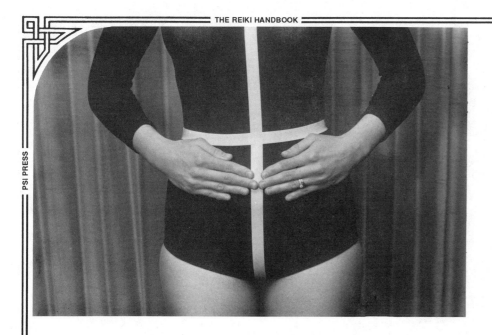

FRONT 2: (Self)

_____

_____

_____

_____

Notes: _____

_____

_____

_____

_____

_____

_____

_____

_____

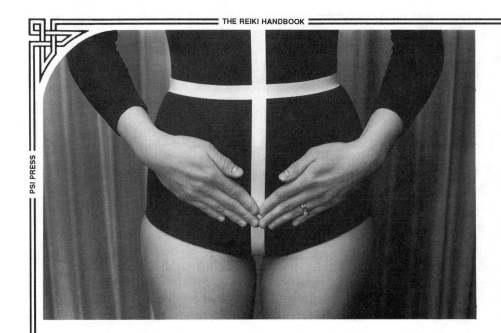

FRONT 3: (Self)

_____

_____

_____

_____

Notes: _____

_____

_____

_____

_____

_____

_____

_____

_____

PSI PRESS

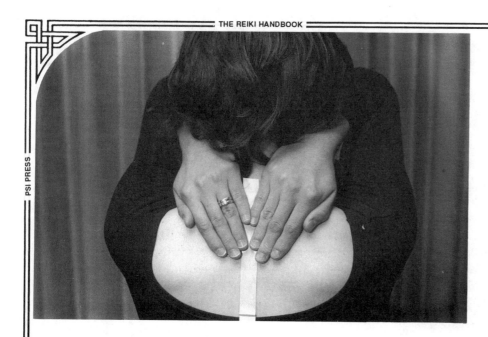

BACK 1: (Self)

_____

_____

_____

_____

Notes: _____

_____

_____

_____

_____

_____

_____

_____

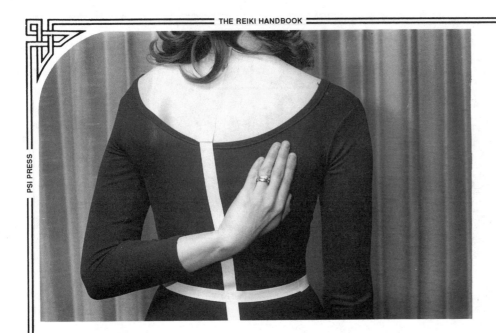

BACK 2: (Self)

_____

_____

_____

_____

Notes: _____

_____

_____

_____

_____

_____

_____

_____

_____

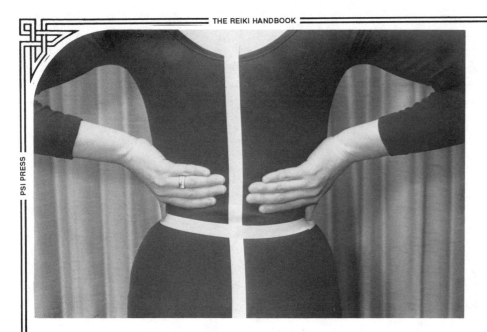

BACK 3: (Self)

_____

_____

_____

_____

Notes: _____

_____

_____

_____

_____

_____

_____

_____

_____

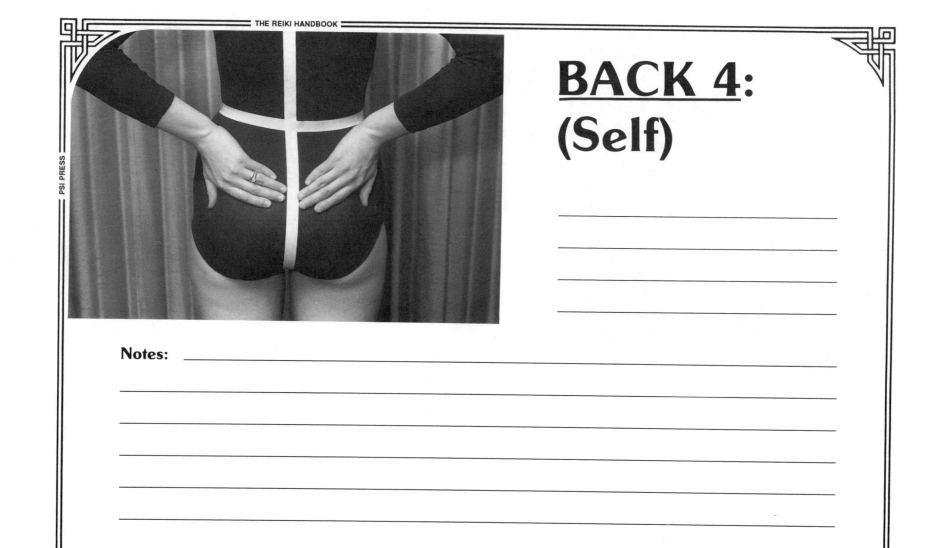

BACK 4: (Self)

_____

_____

_____

_____

Notes: _____

_____

_____

_____

_____

_____

_____

_____

PSI PRESS

HEAD 1: (Other)

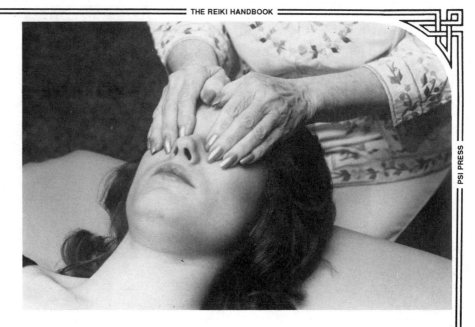

_____

_____

_____

_____

Notes: _____

_____

_____

_____

_____

_____

_____

_____

_____

HEAD 2: (Other)

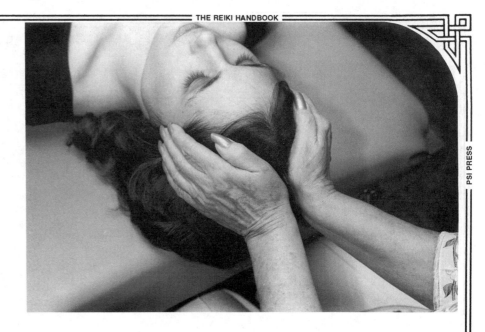

_____

_____

_____

_____

Notes: _____

_____

_____

_____

_____

_____

_____

_____

_____

HEAD 3: (Other)

_____

_____

_____

_____

Notes: _____

_____

_____

_____

_____

_____

_____

_____

_____

HEAD 4: (Other)

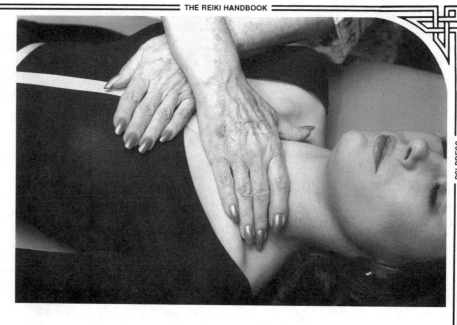

PSI PRESS

_____

_____

_____

_____

Notes: _____

_____

_____

_____

_____

_____

_____

_____

FRONT 1:
(Other)

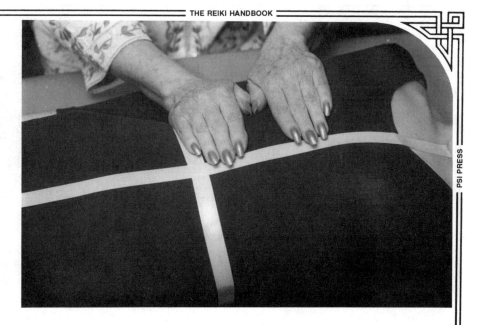

PSI PRESS

_____

_____

_____

_____

Notes: _____

_____

_____

_____

_____

_____

_____

_____

FRONT 2: (Other)

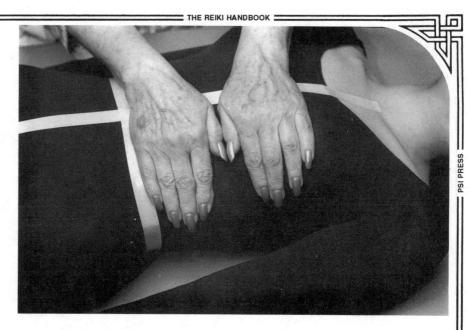

PSI PRESS

_____

_____

_____

_____

Notes: _____

_____

_____

_____

_____

_____

_____

_____

<u>FRONT 3:</u>
(Other)

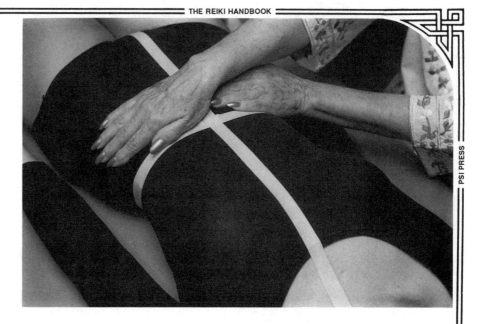

_____

_____

_____

_____

Notes: _____

_____

_____

_____

_____

_____

_____

_____

_____

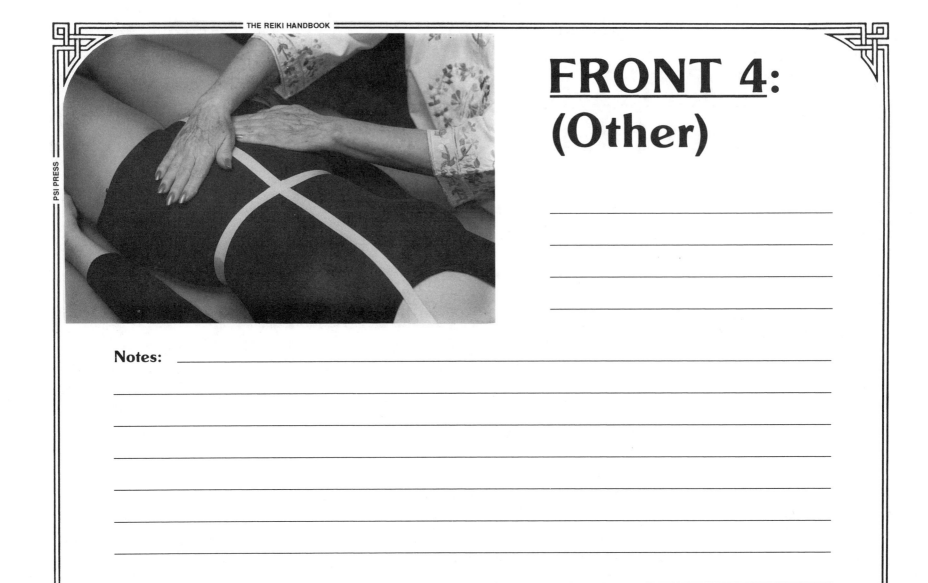

FRONT 4: (Other)

_____

_____

_____

_____

Notes: _____

_____

_____

_____

_____

_____

_____

_____

_____

FRONT 5:
(Other)

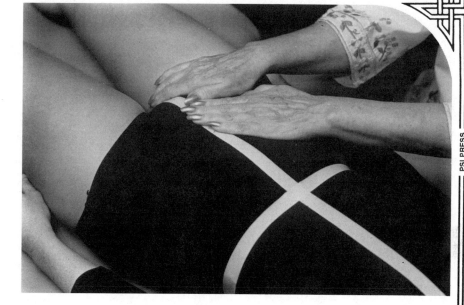

PSI PRESS

_____

_____

_____

_____

Notes: _____

_____

_____

_____

_____

_____

_____

_____

_____

_____

PSI PRESS

BACK 1:
(Other)

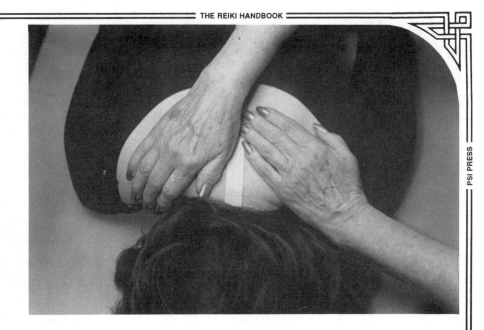

_____

_____

_____

_____

Notes: _____

_____

_____

_____

_____

_____

_____

_____

_____

BACK 2: (Other)

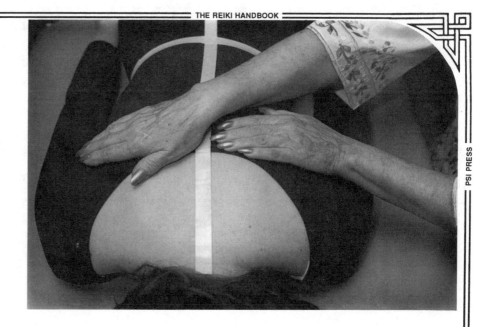

PSI PRESS

_____

_____

_____

_____

Notes: _____

_____

_____

_____

_____

_____

_____

_____

PSI PRESS

BACK 3:
(Other)

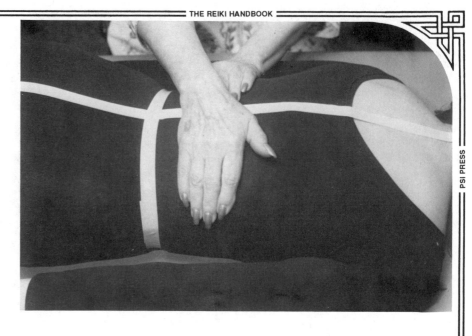

_____

_____

_____

_____

Notes: _____

_____

_____

_____

_____

_____

_____

_____

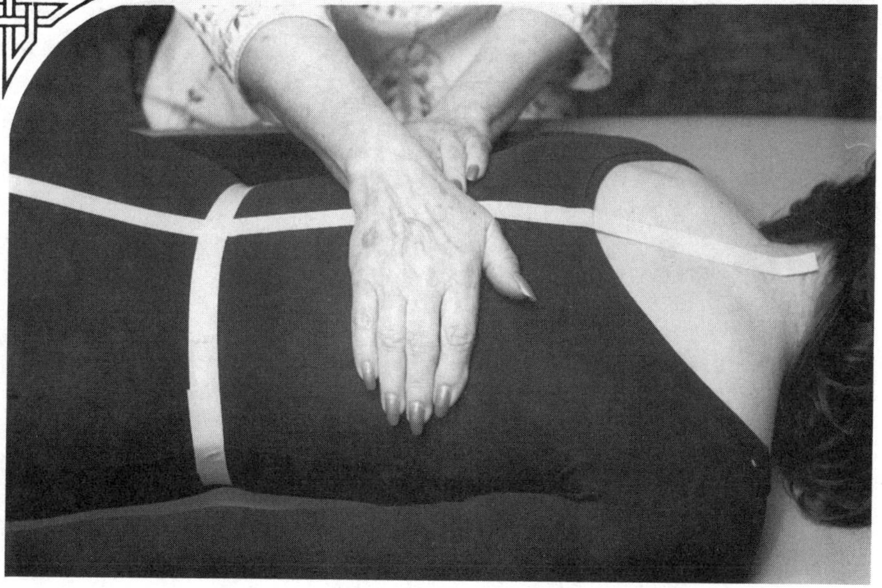

BACK 3A: (Other)

_____

_____

_____

_____

Notes: _____

_____

_____

_____

_____

_____

_____

_____

BACK 4: (Other)

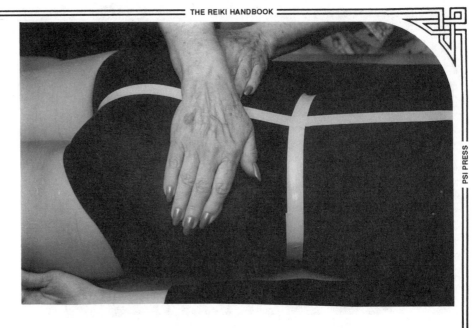

_____

_____

_____

_____

Notes: _____

_____

_____

_____

_____

_____

_____

_____

_____

PSI PRESS

BACK 5:
(Other)

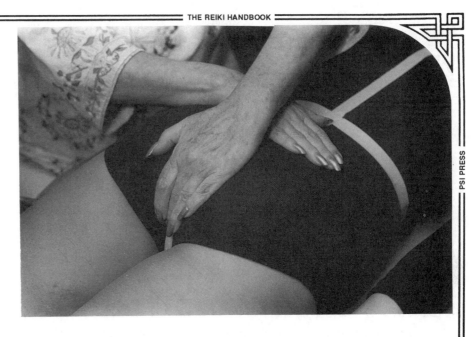

_____

_____

_____

_____

Notes: _____

_____

_____

_____

_____

_____

_____

_____

_____

_____

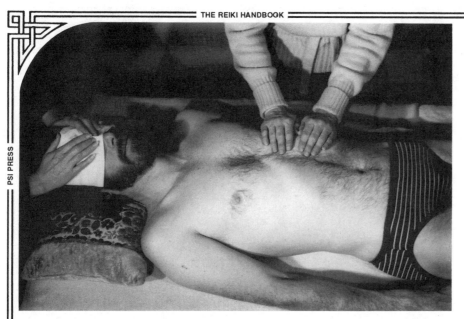

Team Treatment for Diabetes (HEAD # 1 & FRONT # 2)

TEAM TREATMENT:

Notes: _____
_____
_____
_____
_____

PSI PRESS

SPECIAL TREATMENTS:

Notes: _____

_____

_____

_____

_____

_____

_____

_____

_____

_____

_____

_____

_____

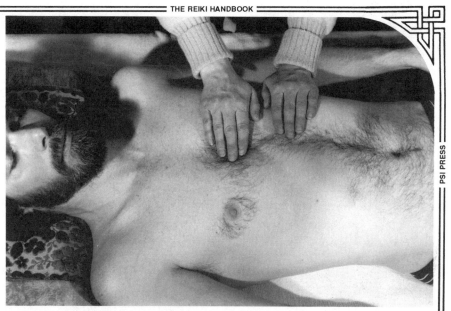

ABOVE: Heart attack.   BELOW: Pleurisy.

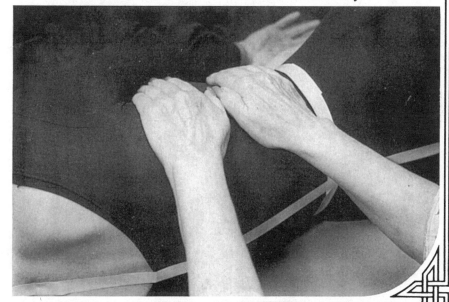

SPECIAL TREATMENTS:

Notes: _____
_____
_____
_____
_____
_____

BELOW: Ears.

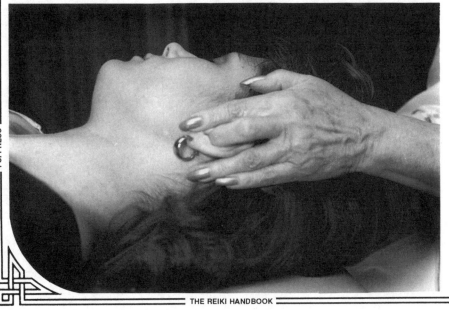

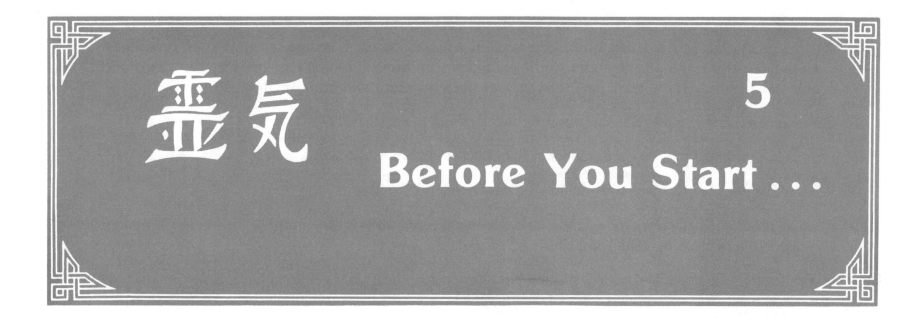

Before You Start . . .

5

By now your instructor and this workbook have guided you through all the criteria necessary for you to utilize Reiki in healing.

You have received the power transfers and are ready to apply this ancient art of effective natural healing to all life-forms that present themselves to you.

Be prepared for surprises!

People, animals and situations you never expected to encounter will be 'mysteriously' attracted to what can benefit them — *you*.

Likewise, you will find yourself equally drawn to those in need. Sometimes this will happen under the seemingly most serendipitous or coincidental of circum-stances. But: on the subconscious level need attracts fulfillment. And one's need for healing, plus your desire to share through Reiki, brings a mutual fulfillment in this exchange-based reality known as life.

As you begin to work with Reiki, particularly upon others, the following review points on procedure will help you establish confidence as well as a respected profes-sionalism and easy rapport with those whom you treat.

These points are listed in the order in which they would normally be encountered during the course of a complete Reiki treatment:

✓ Ask the prospective client when a treatment session is first requested if he can schedule a series of 3 or 4 consecutive daily appointments in the event additional treatments might be required for other than basic health maintenance. Try to book the initial session when this can be accomplished.

✓ Create an environment as quiet, comfortable and soothing as possible.

✓ Place a box of kleenex tissue and a sheet or light blanket within easy reach.

✓ Remind the client of the need to complete the flow of energy exchange.

✓ Remove the client's glasses, shoes, jacket, vest, tie, belt, scarves, and jewelry around the neck. Have pockets emptied. No terribly snug pants, or girdles and pantyhose.

✓ Have the client lie down if possible, placing pillows under his head (or neck) and knees.

✓ Check to confirm the patient's feet are not crossed.

✓ Ask about any known ailments and any major surgery that the patient has experienced.

✓ Remind the patient he may feel worse after the first treatment and, if so, that a minimum of 3 consecutive daily treatments will be required.

✓ Wash your hands with soap and water before beginning the treatment.

✓ Keep your fingers together during treatment.

✓ Aside from emergency situations, always give the Whole Body treatment before focusing on particular ailments for additional Reiki.

✓ Never diagnose or prescribe unless you hold an M.D.

✓ REMEMBER: "Reiki is simple. Reiki is doing what's natural."

"You pick up nothing from the client. Everything goes from you to them."

"Always use Reiki with common sense."

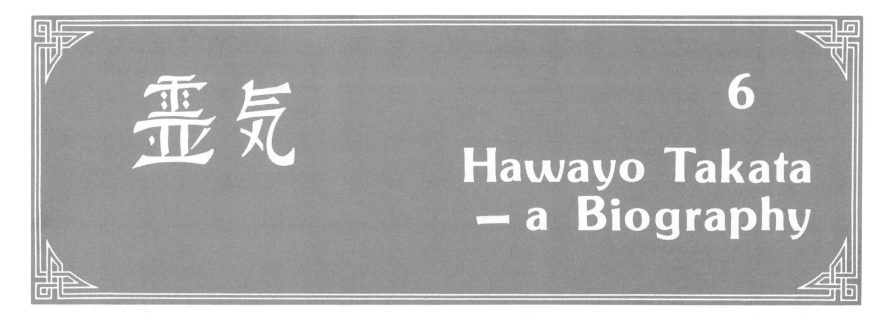

6
Hawayo Takata
— a Biography

Dr. Mikao Usui's rediscovering the keys to Reiki is recounted in Chapter One. However, were it not for the determination of one woman the Usui system of natural healing would probably still be practiced only in Japan. Rather, it is today spreading health throughout the world.

The woman responsible is Hawayo K. Takata.

On December 24, 1900, a second daughter was born in Hawaii to two sugar cane workers of Japanese descent and culture. As the golden sun rose that day out of the waters of the Pacific, her mother instructed the midwife: "Take the infant out into the sunrise. Name this child Hawayo after the big island. Then her name will be important and she will become a worthy person."

Decades later that prophecy would be fulfilled.

As a child, Hawayo's formal education ended at the second grade. She then trained to be the house servant for an accountant, Saichi Takata, at one of Hawaii's plantations. Love entered the arrangement, and the accountant married his servant girl.

Mrs. Takata's life seemed established and routine in the Oriental tradition: a loving husband and two daughters to nurture.

But at age 31, Mrs. Takata was widowed.

Responsibility to care not only for her growing children but her parents too fell upon her frail shoulders. The burden began to break her health, and eventually she needed gall bladder surgery. Always hesitant to trust anyone she didn't know, Mrs. Takata faced the dilemma of knowing physicians only in a Tokyo clinic where her husband had once been a patient. She decided that is where she must go, hardships of the long trip notwithstanding.

When Mrs. Takata's saved pennies totaled $50, she and her daughters booked passage on a cattle boat to Tokyo. Not surprisingly, she was too weak upon arrival at the clinic there to undergo surgery. For six months the Takata family lived at the clinic until she was strong enough for an operation.

Then a strange thing happened.

On the morning for her surgery, as Mrs. Takata lay on the operating table while doctors scrubbed and nurses bustled about, she heard a voice mysteriously speak to her: "Operation not necessary."

She looked around, seeing no one who could be talking to her. "I'm losing my mind," she whispered to herself; "I am hearing strange voices."

Just as she convinced herself it was her imagination, it came again: "Operation *not* necessary."

She tried to persuade herself that she was sleeping or anesthetized, then admitted to herself that she was fully conscious. The voice came a third time: *"Operation not really necessary!"*

"Then what am I to do?" she asked mentally.

"Ask the doctor," replied the voice.

Taking a stance uncharacteristic for a woman raised in the Japanese tradition, Mrs. Takata faced her doctor and declared bluntly: "I don't think this operation is really necessary. There must be a better way. Is there any kind of therapy or a treatment that I can receive and try that you think will help me?"

The doctor, taken aback by this shocking challenge from the petite woman on whom he was to begin surgery, recovered his composure and thought a few moments.

"Yes," he answered. "How long can you remain in this country?"

"I can stay two years," something prompted Mrs. Takata to say.

"Wonderful," replied the surgeon. "If you have two years, wonderful. There *is* a better way!"

He turned to a nurse, instructing her to telephone his sister in the clinic's kitchen. His sister's ailment had been cured by another physician in Tokyo, one who administered drugless and bloodless treatments.

"Take Mrs. Takata to Shimano Machi," he told his sister without hesitation.

Now, after more than three decades, the long-ago prophecy made by Hawayo Takata's mother was unfolding.

En route to the clinic where Machi worked, Mrs. Takata's guide eagerly spoke about her own physical healing there as they rode among Tokyo's maze of streets in a cab. Soon they arrived at the eight-bed clinic and met some of its sixteen practitioners, all managed by Dr. Chugiro Hyashi. Any lingering doubts Mrs. Takata had were quickly dispelled by the warmth of Dr. Hyashi's smile and the hospitality of Mrs. Hyashi.

"Yes," he assured Mrs. Takata, "I can help you."

Mrs. Takata's health began returning as she continued treatments under the hands of Dr. Hyashi and his staff.

But some things perplexed her. How were these healers able to tell her about pains in her body merely through touching — and sometimes even *without* touching — her body, she wondered. And why were the hands of the practitioners so warm — even hot — when touching her, she puzzled.

She reasoned that batteries and electric heaters were hidden underneath the treatment tables. One day she looked for them everywhere in the room, but found nothing.

The batteries that warm the healers' hands must be concealed in their kimonos, she then concluded.

Slyly waiting until a practitioner began treating her, Mrs. Takata grabbed the sleeve of his kimono and, as she ran her hand over his forearm, demanded to know "Where do you keep the batteries that heat your hands?"

The practitioner, perplexed, insisted he had no batteries. Mrs. Takata persisted: there *must* be batteries to generate the warmth she always found so comforting and healing, yet so mysterious.

"No batteries!" This time it was Dr. Hyashi who spoke. Mrs. Takata could not doubt the word of this honorable man who was restoring her body to health and vitality.

The warmth?

"It is this great power we use," said the doctor simply. And he began telling her about Reiki.

"I must have this power," Mrs. Takata told him. "I must have this power."

Mrs. Takata insisted that she be trained in Reiki.

Dr. Hyashi said no. Healing is a man's domain, he countered, a domain which in Japan specifically banned women — *especially* women of the poor lower class.

Mrs. Takata persisted. Dr. Hyashi resisted. It seemed he wanted this natural healing system exclusively for Japan, despite the fact it is based on universal life energy, and feared that Mrs. Takata would 'export' Reiki when she returned home to Hawaii.

Mrs. Takata persevered. "I will have Reiki," she would plead. "I have the responsibility of two parents and two children and I am a poor widow. I must return to Hawaii. There is no way I can come to Japan for treatment. I must be healthy. How am I going to take care of everybody if I don't have Reiki? If I have my health, I have everything; if I do not have my health, I don't have anything. So what are you going to do? Send me off to die somewhere? I must have Reiki!"

Dr. Hyashi relented at last. It was the Spring of 1936. And Hawayo Takata, the American daughter of obscure Japanese sugar cane cutter parents, became the first non-Japanese and first woman in modern times to be certified in the Usui system of Reiki healing.

It was an accomplishment that triumphed over nearly insurmountable odds; an achievement that she could never have dreamed of as a young girl whose cultural heritage did not condone (let alone encourage) tradition-shattering breakthroughs for women.

Mrs. Takata returned home to Hawaii, where she diligently applied herself to first-degree Reiki. In six months she had healed herself and her family. She now felt ready for second-degree Reiki which, as Dr. Hyashi had explained, would enable her to perform absentee healing and also to treat mental problems.

But how could she achieve this desire? Dr. Hyashi was in Japan, and Mrs. Takata could not afford to return there. Besides, convincing the Oriental doctor to give her, a female, the first-degree Reiki had been difficult enough. So how much *more* challenging could obtaining the second-degree be ...

Again, fate (or synchronicity) intervened at a pivotal moment in Mrs. Takata's life.

She knew Dr. Hyashi's daughter was betrothed and that, once married, a Japanese girl remained house-bound for the rest of her life. Mrs. Takata contrived a clever ruse.

She wrote a letter inviting Dr. Hyashi's daughter to visit her in Hawaii prior to the wedding ceremony. The youthful daughter could not be allowed to travel unescorted, of course, and Mrs. Takata knew that Mrs. Hyashi could not leave the family house. The invitation meant, therefore, that the doctor must chaperon his daughter or deny her altogether a fantastic trip to Hawaii.

Mrs. Takata waited; hoped; feared. One day a letter arrived from Japan. She opened it with fingers trembling from expectation combined with apprehension. She knew it came from Dr. Hyashi, but how did he respond to her invitation?

The man to whom the Reiki system had been taught by Dr. Usui himself agreed to permit his betrothed daughter a visit with Mrs. Takata in Hawaii. And, he would be accompanying her!

During the subsequent months of the Hyashis' stay with Mrs. Takata, she convinced the doctor to certify her in second-degree Reiki. Dr. Hyashi saw the depth of his student's commitment to healing, and he was (in the stoic way of the Oriental) pleased with Mrs. Takata's devotion to alleviating the ailments of others.

He was not surprised, then, when one day Mrs. Takata asked to know everything about the discoveries Dr. Usui had made in his own life's quest for a simple natural healing process, discoveries passed on to her own mentor.

"How badly to you want to know?" Dr. Hyashi questioned.

"Worse than anything," Mrs. Takata replied immediately. "It is the most important aspect of my life. Sick people in Hawaii need healing. They can't come to Japan for Reiki. Somebody has to care. I care. Give me more Reiki."

Dr. Hyashi knew better than to say no again to this determined woman. Upon reaching an agreement for the exchange of value that Usui held to be so important, Hawayo Takata became a Reiki Master — the last one initiated by Hyashi himself. It was the Winter of 1938.

The years passed, and the exchange Mrs. Takata made for Reiki and her dedication to healing bountifully blessed her with a rewarding life.

Along with verbal thanks from those healed, some grateful healees bestowed lucrative financial advice as their fair exchange. Consequently Mrs. Takata was able to parlay her meager earnings into valuable real estate holdings, and she became independently wealthy. Sometimes a prepaid airplane ticket would arrive by mail, and she would travel the world administering Reiki.

Never could she as a child have fantasized doing what she did now as the result of Reiki!

Then just before World War II, Dr. Hyashi called Mrs. Takata. He clairvoyantly foresaw the approaching war, and knew that as a reserve admiral in the Japanese Navy he would be inducted into the conflict.

"My mission in life is healing, not death," he spoke solemnly. "I cannot serve in the Japanese Navy. It is time to make my transition. Come to me."

Mrs. Takata soon arrived in Tokyo, where Dr. Hyashi gave her a list of persons to be invited to his farewell. This honor Mrs. Takata performed, and on the appointed day all the guests had gathered and Dr. Hyashi knelt before them.

He talked with his friends; of their commitment to healing their fellowmen, of the good they had seen Reiki do, of the need to do more because suffering would increase dramatically with the onset of war. To Mrs. Takata, he then bequeathed the position of Reiki Grand Master, along with the house that served as a Reiki clinic.

Telling those gathered goodbye, Dr. Hyashi closed his eyes. "I have broken my aorta," he whispered with his last breath on May 10, 1941.

The man who dedicated his life to healing administered upon himself what some consider to be the ultimate act of healing.

Mrs. Takata carried on the legacy of Drs. Usui and Hyashi, applying and spreading the power of Reiki.

During 1974-1976 her hands and words imparted Reiki to Virginia Samdahl, making her the first Occidental in 2,500 years to become a Reiki Master and administer Reiki as rediscovered in the ancient Sanskrit *sutras*.

In December, 1980, Hawayo Takata made her physical transition.

And as did her own spirit in life, Reiki likewise grows stronger each day in restoring health, harmony and happiness to a suffering world.

"The wish for healing has ever been the half of health."
— Seneca, *Hippolytus* (1st Century)

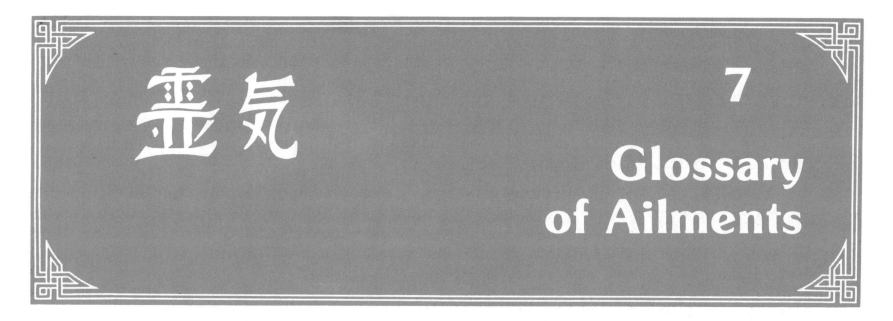

7

Glossary of Ailments

This section lists ailments that the Reiki therapist is likely to encounter, and the most effective treatment procedures. Listings are alphabetical, for easy referral during a Reiki session. Boldface within a listing indicates cross-references to other ailments.

Except in emergency situations, all that follows should be used in conjunction with and after administering a normal Whole Body treatment of HEAD, FRONT and BACK positions.

Space is provided for you to note additional items.

ACCIDENT (general injury) — Treat the solar plexus (over the navel). Then to stabilize the body, treat BACK # 3A (over the adrenals).

ACNE — Spend additional time on FRONT # 3 (stomach area), then the affected areas.

ADHESIONS — Place hands over the afflicted area to release adhesions. Reiki will not heal anything severed by surgery, such as fallopian tubes or nerves in the ear. However, Reiki will help ease post-operative pain and stimulate the body's own healing processes, as well as eliminating shock.

AGING — In addition to general good health practices and Reiki self-treatment, if the client is over 40 years old suggest taking 1000 units of vitamin E, a multiple B-complex, and 1000-and-up milligrams of rose hips vitamin C daily.

ALLERGIES — Allergies, along with **ASTHMA, BRONCHITIS** and **EMPHYSEMA**, result from a basic cause: the lungs never cleared from childhood bronchitis. They are all mucus-related ailments; therefore, mucus-producing foods should first be removed from the diet — including cow's milk products, white sugar, flour, chocolate, carbonated beverages, and red meats.

Treat FRONT # 1, # 2, # 3, # 4, then the top of the lungs. Treat pleura (the delicate membrane lining the thorax) by gently rolling the client on his side, placing both hands on the side of his torso for 30 minutes; roll patient onto his other side, and repeat. Finally, have client lie on his chest and use BACK # 2. For **ALLERGIES**, begin treatment with HEAD # 1. For **ASTHMA**, treat client for 21 consecutive days; for **EMPHYSEMA**, 30 consecutive days. Also, suggest the client employ breathing exercises.

NOTE: If consecutive treatments are not possible, *don't begin.*

ANEMIA — Treat the spleen. Suggest eating all the Reiki slaw possible (see Chapter 9), and drink the Blood Replenisher juice (see Chapter 9) as the complete diet for 7 days.

ANOREXIA NERVOSA — This hysterical condition of extreme loss of appetite or revulsion to food requires second-degree Reiki, since the mind as well as the body must be treated.

ARTHRITIS — Arthritis is related to **BURSITIS, GOUT**, and **RHEUMATISM**. It derives from an inactive bladder, allowing urine retention that causes a uric acid condition in the body, which in turn causes calcium to deposit in the joints. Treat FRONT # 1, # 2, # 3, # 4 with extra time on FRONT # 4 (the bladder area). Then treat BACK # 3 (the kidney area) longer than usual. Then treat the afflicted areas of the body until the calcium breaks down and can be removed by the renal system. Suggest the client drink ½ gallon of water daily, to aid flushing of excess uric acid from the body.

NOTE: If distilled rather than spring water is used, suggest the client maintain his mineral intake at proper levels with supplements.

ASTHMA — See "**ALLERGIES**".

BACK PAIN — For pain in the small of the back, treat FRONT # 3 and # 4, and suggest eating Reiki slaw. For *severe* back injuries, begin by thoroughly treating the back and sides of the neck and then move hands down the back at hand-width intervals. (In the female, lower back pain can result from a tipped uterus. Refer to "**MENSES**".)

BALDNESS — Reiki, in conjunction with diet, has been successful in regenerating growth of hair. Treat the head by placing hands over the bald spots. Protein intake should be increased, and vitamin E oil massaged into the scalp. Also suggest the client consume two cups of soy milk daily instead of taking spirulina, ideally one cup at 10 A.M. and the second at 4 P.M. (Soy beans may be eaten daily in lieu of the soy milk.) See also "**HAIR**".

NOTE: This treatment will likely require patience and dedication. In once instance it took 12 months before hair reappeared, but reappear it did!

BED WETTING — The bladder is weak. Treat FRONT # 4. Have the client strengthen his sphincter muscle by starting to urinate, stop, start and stop several times during each urination.

BEE STINGS/INSECT BITES — Check immediately for venom sack or stinger, or insect's mandibles, and if embedded in skin remove it quickly without tearing the flesh.   Suck gently on wound for 30 seconds, spitting out venom. Place one hand upon wound, and cup other hand (if available) around the limb *or* on the body above the other hand (so that it will come between the wound and flow of blood towards the heart). Maintain for 20 minutes minimum to reduce toxic reaction and swelling. If toxic reaction is particularly virulent, also treat the lymph areas (sides of neck, under the arms, and the groin).

BELL'S PALSY — The cause of this sudden idiopathic unilateral facial paralysis is unknown. Treat HEAD #1, # 2, # 3, cheeks, mouth, under the jaw and behind the ears.

BLEEDING GUMS, MOUTH SORES (HERPES I) — These ailments are often due to excess acidity in one's system, though Herpes I virus seems aggravated by emotional stress. After basic treatment, place hands over the mouth and along sides of the client's face.

Also suggest that sugar, excessive proteins and acid-producing items such as pineapples, citrus fruits and tomatoes be eliminated from the diet until the condition clears. Grapefruit, lemons and peaches have an alkaline effect and can still be eaten. Supplement with rose hips vitamin C.

BRAIN DAMAGE & TUMOR — "Your hands will tell you where to spend the greatest time," says Mrs. Samdahl. In general, devote much time to treating the head and sides of the neck to promote circulation and an adequate blood supply. Also suggest the Blood Replenisher juice.

BREAST LUMPS — Treat FRONT # 4 for 20 minutes, as the ovaries are always involved (even if they've been removed). Then treat the breasts for an additional 20 minutes.

BROKEN BONES — Treat immediately. Place the hands around the break, if possible. The bones will often realign themselves, the pain and swelling will be greatly reduced, and almost no bruising will occur. After the break has been set and cast, treat through the cast.

BRONCHITIS — See "ALLERGIES".

BURNS (minor) — Place hands over the area immediately to prevent blistering. Hold the injury until the pain goes away.

CALLUSES & CORNS — These conditions might result from maladjustments of the spine and/or potassium deficiency. Suggest chiropractic treatment in addition to Reiki. Emphasize BACK # 1, # 2, # 3, # 4, and add 1 tsp. Heinz apple cider vinegar in a glass of water to the client's daily diet.

CANCER — Full treatment, and affected areas for 20-30 minutes. If the client is undergoing chemotherapy, Reiki can only help with alleviating pain and nausea. No healing can take place during this killing process.

For edema and pain in the arm following mastectomy, suggest the client increase vitamin B-6 by 4 per day and water intake by ½ gallon, and eat Reiki slaw to remove toxins; treat underarm, full arm, and in the area of surgery.

CIRCULATION/BLOOD REPLENISHER — Ask the client to lie on his back, with knees bent and legs slightly spread. Place the middle finger of one hand in the groin area over the large artery going to the leg; place the other hand on FRONT # 4 on the same side of the body. Repeat for the other side. If diabetes is involved, spend 30 minutes on FRONT # 2 (over the pancreas). If the client reports loss of feeling in the feet, treat the knees and feet as well.

Suggest the client begin taking 500-1000 milligrams of rose hips vitamin C daily, and slowly increase to 5000 units or more — as much as can be tolerated without causing diarrhea; also 50 milligrams of a balanced vitamin B supplement, and 2000 units of vitamin E daily.

COLDS — Treat FRONT # 1, #2, #3, # 4; upper lungs; then pleura along the sides of the torso, head and back. Three days of consecutive treatment is recommended.

COLIC — Place baby's face down, putting one hand under its stomach and the other upon its back. Hold until gas is released and baby goes to sleep.

NOTE: Colic is a medical term often used to describe whatever ails a new-born when a specific cause cannot be identified; disappearing within three months of birth, it remains a medical mystery. Growing evidence suggests that cow's milk protein may play a developmental role. Beyond that, in 1992 physicians recommend less stimulation; more soothing for the colicky baby. The Reiki treatment given above predates by a decade this recommendation.

COUGHS & PLEURISY — Treat FRONT # 1, # 2, # 3, # 4, upper lungs, HEAD # 4, and pleura.

CONGENITAL DEFECTS (inherited) — Birth defects can be helped by Whole Body treatment if begun when the child is young, but are seldom cured. Neo-natal treatments have a better chance of life-long success. Ideally, treatment should begin in the fetal stage as soon as defects are ascertained in the mother's womb by medical science. See also "**PREGNANCIES**".

REMEMBER: "Babies" — and that includes fetuses — "are wide open to God's love," says Mrs. Samdahl.

CRAMPS — See "MENSES".

CYSTS & BOILS — Apply Whole Body treatment, then focus on the affliction. Place kleenex tissue over the area to absorb secretions when the cyst or boil ruptures. If treatment is begun at the first sign of soreness, the boil or sty often will be re-absorbed into the body. Cysts may be re-absorbed also.

CUTS — Grasp and treat the injured area to seal the opening and stop bleeding. Then clean the cut, bandage it and treat again. Cuts usually require much time to heal, so treat as often as possible.

DEAFNESS — See "EARS".

DETACHED RETINA — Treat HEAD # 1. See also "**EYES**".

DIABETES — Treat FRONT # 2 (over pancreas) for 30 minutes. If the client has limited vision or diabetic blindness, spend extra time on FRONT # 4 (over the ovaries) or BACK # 5 (the prostate), and HEAD # 1.

NOTE: If the client takes insulin, insist that he receive a blood check by a physician each week during Reiki to avoid insulin shock — as the body begins to heal it needs less insulin.

IMPORTANT: When diabetes or diabetic tendencies are present, *do not draw your fingers down the spine*. Instead, when massaging the spine to cleanse the blood, make a V-shape with the forefinger and middle finger and *pull up* along the sides of the spinal column.

DIVERTICULOSIS — Spend extra time on FRONT # 3 and # 4.

DROPPED FOOT — Have the client lie on his back, bend his knees slightly and spread his legs. Place the middle finger on the groin area, and place your other hand on FRONT # 4 on the same side of the abdomen. Then treat the afflicted ankle and foot.

DRUG ADDICTION/OVERDOSE — The client must be in a withdrawal program or treatment is a waste of time. For overdose, *first* treat BACK # 3A (over the adrenals), then Whole Body treatment. Second-degree Reiki is recommended, because in addiction the mind must be treated along with the body.

EARS — Lift the flaps of the ear canals, gently place the middle finger in each ear and rest the hands along sides of client's head behind the ears; the forefingers and thumbs will be to the front of the ears and on the temples, respectively. If the ears are too sore to touch, cup the hands over the ears — "This won't work as fast," says Mrs. Samdahl, "but eventually will be just as effective."

EAR ACHE — Reiki melts the wax blockage and relieves pressure on the inner ear.

DEAFNESS — In addition to the above, treat under the jaws. Results are generally slow. Nerve deterioration can be repaired, but broken eardrums do not respond well to Reiki; nor will Reiki counteract damage from ear surgery.

BLEEDING EARS or VIRAL INFECTIONS — Same as above.

AIRPLANE CABIN PRESSURE — Same as above … middle finger in ear, et cetera.

EDEMA — To dismiss fluid retention in the body, treat FRONT # 4 and over the bladder, then BACK # 3 and # 3A (over kidneys and the adrenals). Suggest the client drink a minimum of 1 large glass or water per day and, since parsley is a good diuretic, eat a bunch of fresh parsley daily or drink 4 to 8 cups of parsley tea. (Vitamin B-6, thyme, and rosemary are also excellent diuretics.)

EMPHYSEMA — See "**ALLERGIES**".

ENERGIZING & REBALANCING — Hold the soles of the client's feet. Place one of your hands upon the client's navel and the other just above it, which tends to rebalance and calm frazzled nerves and emotions. Treat the adrenals and HEAD # 4 (thyroid) to balance metabolism.

NOTE: Holding the soles of a baby's feet will aid the infant grow strong and healthy.

EPILEPSY & CONVULSIVE DISORDERS — Treat HEAD # 1.

EYES — Eye defects such as strabismus (cross-eye), detached retina, and glaucoma usually correspond to problems in the pancreas, thyroid, ovaries, or prostate. Ask if the client has problems in these organs, and treat accordingly.

Also ask the client to perform a simple eye exercise: move the eyeballs from the upper left corner to the upper right corner, then down, across to the left, and up to the left corner again, then to the center, and rest; reverse this pattern. That is, move both eyes in a simple clockwise square first, then in a counterclockwise square. Do this exercise for 5 minutes in the A.M. and 5 minutes in the P.M., working up to 20 minutes twice daily.

NOTE: Use this exercise for strabismus, *never* in the case of a detached retina. For a detached retina, treat HEAD # 1.

FEVER — Treat FRONT # 1, # 2, # 3, # 4 first; then upper lungs and sides of the chest to affect the lungs' pleura. Follow with HEAD # 1, # 2, # 3, # 4 and BACK # 1, # 2, # 3, # 4. Remain in each position until the rise-and-fall of energy is felt, perhaps 8 to 10 minutes, longer if necessary.

FOOD POISONING — Treat FRONT # 1, # 2, # 3, # 4; then BACK # 3A and # 4. Drink as much water as possible as soon as the client can keep it down, to overcome dehydration.

FRACTURES — See "BROKEN BONES".

FROSTBITE — If there is not time for Whole Body treatment, treat directly on the afflicted area and then over the adrenals.

GALL BLADDER & LIVER — Hold FRONT # 1 until a release in the gall bladder — a "glug, glug" — is heard. If after 15 minutes it's not heard and energy blockage release is not sensed, ask the client if it has been removed. If the client has gall stones, it may require several hours or several treatments for them to break down and release.

HAIR — To grow hair, use HEAD # 2 placement. Also suggest the client increase his protein intake without increasing his red meat consumption by eating spirulina-plankton, soy milk or soy beans. Massage the scalp firmly in the evening with mineral oil or vitamin E oil; leave on overnight. Wash the hair every morning. See also "**BALD-NESS**".

HANGOVER — Have the sufferer drink as much water as possible. Treat FRONT # 1 and # 2, sides of neck, and HEAD # 1, # 2, # 3.

HEADACHE (migraine) — Eliminate as much as possible sources of heat, light and noise from the room. Treat FRONT # 1, # 2, # 3. As an energy link exists between the migraine center and the ovaries (FRONT # 4) or prostate area (BACK # 5), treat the latter for 30 minutes and then gently place hands over client's eyes (usually aberrant energy can be discerned around the left eye). Treat HEAD # 1, # 2, # 3. Help the client roll over, then treat BACK # 1, # 2, # 3, # 4, and in males BACK # 5. Conclude with a light body massage, then cover the client with a sheet and allow him to rest until ready to get up voluntarily. Suggest he then return home, go directly to bed, and sleep.

NOTE: When migraine lasts two or more days, consecutive treatments will be required.

HEADACHE (tension) — The client will likely have much energy activity around the stomach and over the left shoulder blade where the sympathetic nervous area is. Therefore treat FRONT # 1, # 2, # 3, # 4 ; then massage back of neck. Treat HEAD # 1, # 2, # 3. Then massage back of the neck, pulling up slightly with the fingers on the base of the skull in HEAD # 3 placement to release pressure points. Massage BACK # 1; then treat BACK # 1, # 2, # 3, # 4. Finish with a *firm* massage. Recommend the client then sleep.

HEAD INJURIES — Emphasize the sides of the neck (around the carotid artery) to stimulate circulation and blood supply. Then Whole Body treatment, spending much time on the entire head and BACK # 3A (the adrenals).

HEART ATTACK — This is an emergency situation! Treat *immediately* by placing one hand gently over the heart and the other on FRONT # 2. Attune to a release of gas or breakup of blockage, then follow procedure listed in **"HEART PROBLEMS"**.

HEART PROBLEMS — Never go straight to the heart — except in an emergency. Treat FRONT # 1, then remain longer on FRONT # 2 until gaseous release is discerned. Then go to the heart area, followed by FRONT # 3 and # 4.

HEMATOMA — For swellings filled with extravasated blood, apply Whole Body treatment and then place hands over the afflicted area. The blood will be re-absorbed into client's body. Clots will *not* break loose and go to the heart.

HEMOPHILIA — Treat FRONT # 2 (over the pancreas). Bleeding should stop in about 20 minutes. Encourage that the Blood Replenisher juice be taken. Hemophilia is unlikely to be healed totally.

HEMORRHAGE — Place one hand over the afflicted area, the other over FRONT # 2.

HEMORRHOIDS & RECTAL FISSURES — Treat BACK # 5, lightly placing your middle finger directly over the anus with hand lying between the buttocks, and other hand across the base of the spine. Treat 20-30 minutes, according to the rise-and-fall of Reiki energy.

HICCUPS — Raise the client's hands over his head to stretch his diaphragm. Place one hand on his diaphragm (at the base of the sternum) and the other hand below it. Hold this position until the hiccups stop. Then ask the client to sit up and drink a few sips of tepid water. If the hiccups recur, treat again.

NOTE: It is recommended a container be kept nearby in case of nausea.

HIGH BLOOD PRESSURE — Place hands *lightly* on the sides of the client's neck (slightly to the front) and over the carotid artery. Treat about 20 minutes, according to the rise-and-fall of Reiki energy.

INFECTION — Treat through kleenex directly over the boil, sore, or contaminated area.

NOTE: If the client is suffering from an infection, it is in the blood stream. Therefore, a Whole Body treatment is vital.

INSECT BITES — See "BEE STINGS".

INVERTED NIPPLE — Place hand upon it for about 20 minutes. Several treatments may be necessary.

LARYNGITIS — Place hands directly on the client's throat, holding according to the rise-and-fall of Reiki energy.

LEARNING & MEMORY — To enhance learning and memory recall, spend additional time on HEAD # 2 and the carotid artery.

NOTE: Reflect on the esoteric significance — and subconscious Reiki — of the innate reflex of grasping the head with both hands when crying out "I just don't know *what* to do!"

LISTLESSNESS — Place one hand over the solar plexus (navel) and the other above it. Also treat the soles of the feet. See also "**ENERGIZING & REBALANCING**".

LIVER — See "**GALL BLADDER**".

MASTOIDITIS — This condition is an inflammation of the mastoid process of the temporal bone behind the ear. Treat HEAD # 3 and behind the ears, as for deafness.

MEASLES — For adults, administer Whole Body treatment immediately. For children, apply Whole Body treatment 24 hours after outbreak. Spend extra time over eyes in HEAD # 1.

MEMORY RECALL — See "**LEARNING & MEMORY**".

MENSES/MENSTRUAL CONTRACTIONS — For frontal cramps — which indicate congested ovaries — treat FRONT # 4 over the ovaries. For lower back pain — which often indicates a tilted uterus — treat BACK # 4. Begin treatments 4 to 5 days prior to menses if cramps recur regularly, and treat every day of menses (10 to 12 consecutive days).

MIGRAINE — See "HEADACHE (migraine)".

MOLES & WARTS — Pinch gently between fingers, treating as often as possible. They will dry up and drop off.

MOTION SICKNESS — This dis-ease and nausea results from motion stimulation of the semicircular canals in the ears. Treat FRONT # 1 to get the gall bladder to release (see "GALL BLADDER"). Additionally, treat the balance area on the head: hands above the ears with heel of the palms on temples and fingers around back of the head.

MUCUS EXCESS — Treat longer on HEAD # 1, but place fingertips on the three pressure points along each eyebrow rather than over the eyes themselves. Suggest elimination of cow's milk products, chocolate, and carbonated beverages from the diet. If sinusitis is causing mucus buildup, see "SINUSITIS".

MULTIPLE SCLEROSIS — This is a neurological disease characterized by speech disturbance, muscular incoordination, and weakness due to sclerotic patches in the brain and spinal cord; its cure is as yet undiscovered by medical science. Apply Whole Body treatment for prolonged periods at least once per day, with extra time on the thigh area to improve circulation in the legs. Also, additional emphasis on HEAD placements helps to regulate and stabilize the brain and nerve functioning. Recommend removal of sugar from the diet, and eating many raw fruits and vegetables. "Multiple sclerosis responds slowly," says Mrs. Samdahl, "but it *responds*."

MUMPS — After Whole Body treatment, place hands over client's testicles or ovaries for 30 minutes. The throat, jaws and lymph areas should also be focused on. For adults: begin treatment immediately. For children, begin treatment after 24 hours have elapsed — that is, on the second symptomatic day — so that the child's immune system has the opportunity to build up a natural defense to the disease.

NASAL POLYPS — Place fingers around the nose cartilage for several minutes. After several treatments, the roots will break loose allowing the polyps to come out.

NOSEBLEED — Prop up the client's torso at a 45-degree angle. Hold an ice bag on the back of his neck and with the other hand make a fist with the thumb on top, and press the nose's cartilage between the thumb and first finger to close the nostril opening. If the client is able to use his hands, have him press on both cheekbones just beyond the base of his nose with the first finger of each hand.

OBESITY — "There's one thing you have to learn first: push yourself away from the table!" exclaims Mrs. Samdahl. Then treat the thyroid. Treatment for obesity is more effective with second-degree Reiki.

PANCREATIC PROBLEMS — For pancreas-related ailments like diabetes and hypoglycemia, treat FRONT # 2 until you hear the pancreas gurgle. If vibrations are felt in this position, the client might have diabetes or be prone to it. Don't hastily 'diagnose' diabetes, though; you could be sensing digestive processes in the nearby stomach! Refer also to "**DIABETES**".

NOTE: For hypoglycemia, treat the adrenals and thyroid too.

PARKINSON'S DISEASE — This is a nervous condition characterized by tremors (especially of the fingers and hands), rigidity of muscles, slowness of speech and movement, and mask-like facial expressions. In addition to Whole Body treatment and focusing on afflicted appendages, give a *full* HEAD treatment — that is, place cupped hands over the entire surface of the skull.

PHLEBITIS — See "**VARICOSE VEINS**".

PLANTAR WARTS — These warts on the bottom of the feet should be soaked in warm water for 10 minutes. Then apply 2 to 3 drops of liquid vitamin E to the wart. Cover with a bandage and treat the top and bottom of the foot at the same time for 7 consecutive days, 30 minutes each time. If the wart does not lift out then, continue treatment until it does.

PLEURISY — See "**COLDS**".

PNEUMONIA — Allow the client to rest on pillows in an inclined position if he has trouble breathing. Treat HEAD # 1, # 2, # 3, # 4; then FRONT # 1, # 2, # 3, # 4 along with the sides of the chest. Reach *under* the body to treat BACK # 1, # 2, # 3, # 3A, # 4, # 5. *Never turn the patient on his stomach, as he could choke in his lung fluid.* Once the fever breaks, rinse the client from the feet towards the head with a cool damp towel. Then cover him with a blanket to promote sweating.

NOTE: In crisis conditions, treatments could require 4 to 5 hours until the fever breaks — so team treatment or team members taking turns is advisable. In non-crisis conditions, treat every day until the fever breaks (usually about the fifth day).

PREGNANCY — "Reiki's the greatest thing for pregnancies," asserts Mrs. Samdahl. "It makes a healthy strong baby, and makes deliveries easier. Babies…are wide open to God's love." Treat the expectant mother's FRONT # 1, # 2, # 3, # 3, # 3, # 4; that is, focus on the womb.

PROSTATE GLAND PROBLEMS — See "HEMORRHOIDS" and give additional emphasis to the throat (thyroid gland). "Once a man is 40," instructs Mrs. Samdahl, "the first time he comes to you for a treatment be sure to check his prostate condition." The prostate is the muscular organ that surrounds the urethra of males at the base of the bladder.

PYORRHEA — Also called Rigg's Disease, this ailment is characterized in severe forms by the formation of pus in the pockets between the roots of the teeth and their surrounding tissues, often resulting in loosening and subsequent loss of the teeth themselves. Treat for 5 consecutive days, following Whole Body treatment with placement of hands over jaw bones and teeth as well as under the client's lower jaw. Spend 30 minutes daily on the jaws and mouth. Within 5 days (usually the fifth day) pus from the infection will be emitted from the gums; press firmly with kleenex tissue on the outside of the mouth to raise and further loosen pus in the gums. Have the client rinse his mouth with tepid water and spit out the residue; repeat this procedure several times. Then continue treatments for additional 5 days to tighten gums and seal in teeth.

RADIATION EXPOSURE — Apply Whole Body treatment, followed by additional treatment of the affected area. Be sure to treat the spleen (at the base of the rib cage on the left side).

If radiation exposure was heavy — as from weapons testing, medical overdoses, or nuclear power plant accidents — treatments will be required more than once per day. "The best way to approach [this] situation," recommends Dr. Weber in *The Reiki Review* [II-2, 2], "is to experiment with various amounts of time doing Reiki *each day* and determine what seems to energize you most effectively."

SCARS — Place hands over scar tissue, and repeat treatment often if scars are less than two years old. "After that," says Mrs. Samdahl, "don't expect much."

SHINGLES — This skin disease affects the posterior roots of the peripheral nerves and causes clusters of blisters; also called Herpes. Place hands below the sternum (breast bone) and over the left shoulder blade on the back (nervous center). Then treat all afflicted areas. Cover with tissues; be gentle. The skin is very sensitive and painful.

SICKLE CELL ANEMIA — Channel extra Reiki to the spleen, upper lungs and pleura, liver and heart. Treat the joints. If the person receiving treatment is a family member of if you have unlimited time, treat full length of the arms and legs and cover the entire body since sickle cells have difficulty passing through small arterioles and capillaries (thus causing thrombosis and hematomas).

SINUSITUS — Treat HEAD # 1. Then rest fingers on the three pressure points above each eyebrow. If the maxillary sinuses are affected, place the hands under the eyes and across the cheeks with your fingers on each side of the client's nose. If the frontal sinuses are afflicted, place the fingertips on the three pressure points above each eyebrow on the frontal bone of the skull. Also treat HEAD # 3, which covers the two sinus points on the back of the head.

NOTE: Often sinus problems are related to the lungs, so consider treating FRONT # 1 and # 2. If excess mucus is aggravating the sinuses, suggest the client eliminate all mucus-producing foods from his diet. See "**ALLERGIES**" for details.

SNAKE BITE — Cut the skin at the location of the bite as quickly as possible, using a very sharp edge such as a razor blade. Suck the area several times, spitting out the venom. Place one hand directly over the wound and, if possible, the other hand over the blood vessels between the wound and the heart. If other Reiki therapists are available, treat the lymph system (neck, groin, and under the arms) simultaneously for at least 30 minutes, longer if sensed necessary.

SPINAL PROBLEMS — Treat the back of the neck, sides of the neck, then work the hands down the entire length of the spine one hand-width at a time.

STROKE — *Do not treat the client for 21 days after the stroke* — the blood needs to settle and find new pathways.

Begin treatment on the twenty-second day with FRONT # 1, # 2, # 3, # 4; then spend about an hour on HEAD # 1, # 2, # 3. Devote the greatest time to areas where most activity is sensed. Maintain treatment for 4 consecutive days. If feet and legs are affected, treat as for varicose veins. If hands and arms are affected, treat the armpits, elbows and wrists.

STUTTERING — This is caused by emotional problems that must be treated with second-degree Reiki.

SUNBURN — Treat BACK # 3A (adrenals) and affected areas.

TEETH — See "**BLEEDING GUMS**" and "**PYORRHEA**".

NOTE: This interesting case is described by one Reiki therapist. "Carolyn, 9, fell and broke off her two center front teeth. The dentist tested for nerve damage and declared them dead. I gave her four treatments after which there was feeling in both the upper and lower front teeth, and after testing the dentist declared the nerves to be alive so that the teeth could be capped."

THROAT (sore) — Place hands over front and sides of throat, and lymph areas under the ears. Then treat the client's chest area.

THYROID GLAND PROBLEMS — The thyroid is a master gland that must be in balance for the body to function properly. Place one hand gently at the base of the throat. As the thyroid works in conjunction with the adrenals, they also must be treated; i.e., BACK # 3A.

TIC DOULOUREUX — This is a nerve spasm of the face. Do not touch the skin for the first 3 treatments. Hold hands ¼-inch above the client's skin and treat HEAD # 1, # 2, # 3; then under his chin, and over lips. If marked improvement is noted after the third treatment, contact healing can gently be used thereafter.

TINNITUS (ringing-in-the-ears) — See "**EARS**" and "**DEAFNESS**".

TONGUE (sore or burned) — Treat the soles of the feet, with particular emphasis on applying pressure to the tops of the big toes.

TONSILS — Spend extra time on HEAD # 1, # 2, # 3, and then cup hands under the lower jaw for 10 to 20 minutes according to the rise-and-fall of Reiki energy.

ULCERS — Treat over the painful area. Suggest eating boiled or steamed okra, which is beneficial for ulcers; okra capsules are also helpful. Recommend that the client learns how to handle stress by following the five Reiki principles.

VAGINITIS — Treat with one hand directly over the vagina and the other hand in the middle of the FRONT # 4 position (over the uterus).

VARICOSE VEINS — Place one hand on inside of the afflicted leg where it joins the crotch, and other hand on FRONT # 4. Treat for 20 minutes or more; lesser time may subsequently be necessary for the other leg. If veins are very bad, "sandwich" the knee and ankle areas also.

VENEREAL DISEASES — After Whole Body treatment, spend extra time on the affected areas. For the woman, treat as for vaginitis. For the man, treat directly on the penis and testicles. This in an infection, so spleen and lymph glands must be treated also. Naturally, the therapist must utilize proper hygiene safeguards.

WHIPLASH — Treat back of the neck, sides of the neck, gently massage shoulders, then work down the spine one hand-width at a time.

Notes: _____

_____

_____

_____

Notes: _____

_____

_____

_____

_____

_____

_____

_____

_____

_____

_____

_____

Notes:

8 Pets and Wildlife

Pets, animals and plants have universal life energy too, hence all can be rebalanced and vitalized by Reiki.

Most sick animals will instinctively come to you for healing because they sense you can benefit them. And though animals will generally respond especially well to Reiki, there are distinct variations from the standard Positions and procedures used on people. For the first time in print, these will be discussed in-depth here.

One immediate difference to understand is the need on your part for *commitment* ... and *patience*. Unless you are prepared to incorporate these two requirements into your hands-on Reiki therapy for animals, you are apt to experience some disappointment.

When treating an animal, remember not to excite it by forcing it to accept a particular position. Instead, allow the animal to become comfortable and work around it, or ease it gently into a position where you hands can reach the areas needing treatment. Certainly a table is not necessary; a couch, a bed, or any other place your pet feels secure — including your lap, naturally — is appropriate.

In an *emergency* situation, calm the animal first by using a reassuring voice combined with gentle stroking over the Head (crown) Position. Covering its head helps to calm, too.

Sometimes it is most helpful to have another person working with you — someone with whom the animal is familiar — to do the talking and stroking while you allow the Reiki to do the healing.

REIKI CASE HISTORIES WITH ANIMALS

While similarities to humans certainly exist when applying Reiki to animals, *there are important differences and concerns* the practitioner needs to be aware of in order to minimize distress to the animal and to maximize the treatments' efficacy.

Since few Reiki therapists will be called on to treat elephants or other large, exotic animals, we will focus on techniques for small domestic and wild animals.

A specialist in the healing of small animals is Lewis R. Hartman, D.V.M. He is a graduate of the School of Veterinary Medicine, University of Illinois, and the co-owner of the Animal Hospital of Dauphin County (241 South Hershey Road, Harrisburg, PA 17112-9315). He is perhaps the first Reiki-certified veterinarian in the United States, and as a second-degree Reiki therapist he has incorporated Reiki in his professional practice since Spring 1987.

Does Reiki *really* make a difference with animals? Let's look at a few of his cases.

"Mackey the cat was a very interesting case," recalls Dr. Hartman. "This cat seemed to develop every known ailment-rejection under the sun. We did all the standard testing — feline leukemia, immune deficiencies, everything we could test for that was capable of being tested for. Everything was negative. Yet this cat kept getting repeated infections. It was in-and-out of the hospital with recurrent bladder infections, skin infections, gastrointestinal infections; you name it, it had it!" It looked like a hopeless case, that got even worse —

"After we had it in the hospital for a few days," Dr. Hartman continued, "it went down and was paralyzed in all four legs. Blood work confirmed meningitis, and it was in the spine. No movement in the limbs at all. *By rights, it should have been dead in two days.*

"And that is when I started doing Reiki on it."

Dr. Harman continues: "I did Reiki every night on this cat for a solid two weeks … maybe 1½ hours at a time. And by the time I was done, it was up and walking. Its temperature was normal. Now it was still getting antibiotics, which it was before.

"I think without the Reiki the cat would have died, *without question.*"

Mackey went home with its elated owners, where it spent another eight months living!

"The people were very, very happy to have this cat for that length of time," recalls Dr. Hartman. "After that initial two weeks with meningitis, we sent it home. And it was functional, and it was normal. It was eating. It gained weight. It was a normal cat up to the time it got to get sick again."

That illness, the veterinarian explained, sadly developed when its owners *boarded* their cat. "It basically

---

FACING PAGE: These sketches of feline anatomy will aid you in treating cats' conditions similarly as you would for human beings.

Cat :

LYMPH NODES:

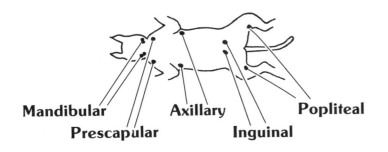

Mandibular Axillary Popliteal
Prescapular Inguinal

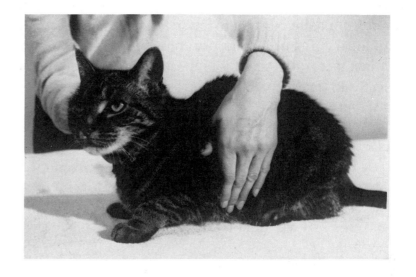

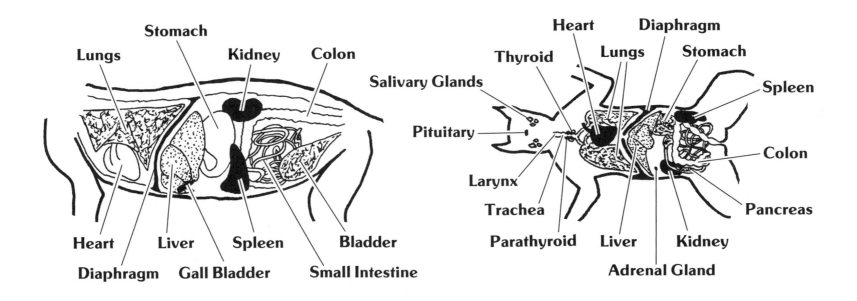

Lungs Stomach Kidney Colon

Heart Liver Spleen Bladder
Diaphragm Gall Bladder Small Intestine

Salivary Glands Thyroid Heart Diaphragm Lungs Stomach Spleen

Pituitary Colon

Larynx Pancreas
Trachea
Parathyroid Liver Kidney
Adrenal Gland

went from being normal to having, 24 hours later, severe pulmonary (upper respiratory) breathing distress — and by then it was too late. I told the staff I was coming in to do a Reiki treatment, but it died about half an hour before I got there."

However, the story of Mackey does not end there, as Dr. Hartman explains:

"When I *was* doing the Reiki, I was concentrating — with the meningitis — along the back for its recurrent bladder infection, and things like that. Not so much the chest area — I was treating it there but not so much as the other areas.

"So interestingly, when the cat did die and I did a post-mortem, the reason for its death was severe pneumonia and collapse of the lungs. It was interesting that it finally took that area to manifest itself and become lethal, and maybe that was the *one* area I didn't treat as much as the others.

"But the cat did have immune deficiency. As Virginia [Samdahl] said, that's one thing you can't cure. A genetic predisposed immune deficiency you aren't going to cure."

Certainly, though, Reiki made a memorable contribution to the life of Mackey. As Dr. Hartman affirms: *This cat lived 6-to-8 months longer!"*

Dr. Hartman points out that the owners of Mackey were "very conducive to what I called 'physical therapy'. To this day, they don't know it was Reiki. (That's a little tip from Virginia!)"

But this veterinarian is completely open about his utilization of Reiki in the clinic.

And was his staff and colleagues supportive?

"One was," he says. "Some of them would make humorous cracks about me 'doing that mumbo-jumbo'."

Whatever one might call Reiki, the bottom line in the veterinarian field is: Does it work? Has it repeatedly been proven effective on non-humans? How might *you* apply this universal life energy when working with animals?

For answers to these questions, let's look at two cases involving German shepherd dogs.

"One German shepherd came in" in the fall of 1987, recounts Dr. Hartman. "I did the x-rays and usual treatment for herniated disk and lower limb paralysis. The spinal cord was being pushed up by the herniated disk and causing the pressure. Instead of the dog getting better with treatment, it was going downhill. Using the standard medical treatment the dog was losing ground, not gaining it.

"So I started doing the Reiki. And there I concentrated on the head, the spine, the back, and the rear legs. I started with the heel of my hand on the crown (overlap my two hands going down the back) for the First Position. Then because it was a German shepherd [large dog], to get my hands around the full circumference of its back, I

FACING PAGE: These sketches of canine anatomy will aid you in treating dogs' conditions similarly as you would for humans beings.

Dog :

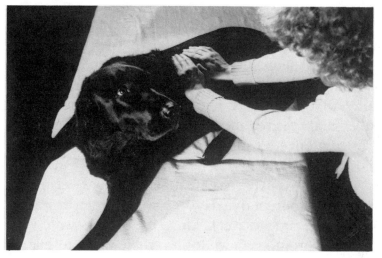

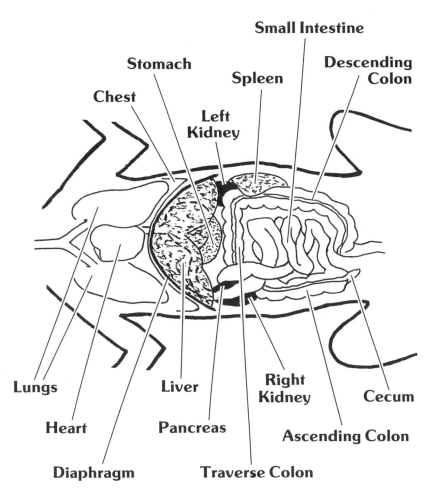

Chest

Stomach

Left Kidney

Spleen

Small Intestine

Descending Colon

Lungs

Liver

Right Kidney

Cecum

Heart

Pancreas

Ascending Colon

Diaphragm

Traverse Colon

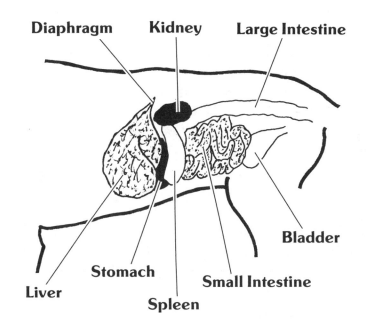

Diaphragm

Kidney

Large Intestine

Liver

Stomach

Spleen

Small Intestine

Bladder

put my hands side-by-side and finished it that way … maybe four positions there.

"I did an additional Position on the rear legs, inside-outside — making sure I placed my hand over the femoral artery and nerve, and making sure the heel of my outside hand covered the back of the legs, and the palm and fingers covered the sciatic nerve (which is on the outside back of the leg).

"That was everyday treatment while it was in the hospital, and consecutive days for seven-to-ten days; and then for three times a week, since the owners were very good about bringing their dog in; then down to once a week."

Three years later, this dog remains quite healthy!

Another German shepherd came to the Animal Hospital of Dauphin County in early 1988, suffering spinal cord damage caused by ruptured disks. The 'patient' was assigned to Dr. Hartman's care.

"That dog had limited use of its rear legs — not completely paralyzed like the first dog — especially the one rear leg. So it was rather isolated. If you'd look at it anatomically, it was isolated to one lateral side of the spinal cord where it was damaged," he explains. He began the Reiki.

"That dog took just as long as the other dog that was completely paralyzed. It didn't seem to be any difference with the healing: it took about the same amount of time

"That dog, to this day [December 1989], is doing well."

REIKI MODIFICATIONS FOR ANIMALS

The Reiki therapist will eventually discover that working hands-on with animals requires some simple (but important!) modifications of technique and outlook.

To aid you in developing proficiency with animals, we offer these insights, based on more than two decades of cumulative experience:

One of many differences when treating animals is the *expediency* with which Reiki must be administered.

Humans have more latitude when manifesting an ailment into their bodies, and generally more time to integrate a rebalancing. Not so with animals.

Reiki — indeed surgery — would be hard-pressed to repair all the nerve damage to the German shepherds described above. But such damage could be minimized — possibly averted — if treatment were administered when symptoms first manifest.

Response time is *crucial* to healing the injuries of animals. The first rule for animals clearly appears to be this: *immediacy of treatment is vital!**

---

* A frightened, injured animal (especially a dog) can be aggressive, making quick treatment difficult. For a *free* copy of "Common Emergencies and Your Dog" — with many helpful hints applicable to animals, generally — write to Ralston Purina, PO Box 88988, Checkerboard Square, St. Louis, MO 63188-1988.

"In both these cases," Dr. Hartman points out about the German shepherds, "the injury or trauma happened several days before I saw the animal. So naturally *if you were there* — if the owner were there and could administer Reiki *right away* — then the initial swelling you could reduce, which would then reduce the permanent damage to the nerve fibers that actually die and are lost.

"So: *speed is of the essence.* You can lose spinal cord tissue in 24 hours, and it [the tissue] can be hopelessly gone."

Terry E. Reed, D.V.M., emphasizes this point too when referring to rabbits, a species the Reiki therapist is apt to encounter because of their increasing popularity as indoor pets.

"Injuries and other maladies of the rabbit will respond to care with a higher degree of proficiency *if the care is immediate* rather than delayed for hours or even days," he writes for the American Rabbit Breeders Association. "If medicants are handy and available, the owners are much more likely to treat the animal *immediately* rather than if they must be purchased and brought back to the rabbitry [home]."

Therefore, a simple first-aid kit should be assembled for the special situations which animals present that human clients do not. At the minimum, the following items are recommended to have close-at-hand:

1) antiseptic — peroxide or equivalent to cleanse infected areas prior to therapy;

2) surgical scissors/forceps — to clip away fur from the infected area;

3) antibiotic creme — for applying to exposed flesh after cleansing; the authors use Betadine and Neosporin;

4) udder balm or thuja ointment — applied atop the antibiotic to keep the wound area soft; to protect against chafing, the authors find Desitin ointment is easy to apply, very efficacious, and harmless to animals if they lick or ingest it.

Speaking of ingesting … acute-care dogs and cats often undergo a radical change in their capacity to metabolize food, even though they may continue eating. If a highly stressed pet does not receive specific nutrients needed by its altered body chemistry, it may be at risk for damage to internal organs within 24 hours, according to veterinary nutritionist Dr. Elizabeth Hodgkins. "Damage is further compounded because many pets in critical care cannot or will not eat on their own," she says.

Therefore, because odds are about 1-in-7 that a domestic dog or cat will be hospitalized with an injury sometime in its life, you should be ready to provide the pet in your care with some of the high-technology, energy-dense pet foods introduced in the early 1990s.*

_____

* Feeding applications of this new food include trauma, surgical recovery, some cancers, chemotherapy, burns, and many systemic diseases. One product is Prescription Diet a/d brand by Hill's (a division of Colgate-Palmolive); 800/445-5777 for information.

Another difference is *pacing* of treatments.

"One thing I found out," says Dr. Hartman, "was that with humans you go the four consecutive days, then start breaking it up to three times a week or something like that. It seems that with animals — specifically with dogs and cats (I don't do large animals, so I don't know about them) — you need to do *consecutive days for as long as you need to, to get substantial improvement. That rule of* four consecutive days *does not hold true.*"

A third difference is the *amount of time* likely required for successful treatment.

"It's not the same as with humans," Dr. Hartman says, based on his three years' experience. "It's definitely a major investment. It's probably easier with a person — because it does takes so long to get a response [with animals, that is]."

A fourth difference is that *acceptance time of Reiki will vary between animal species*, much more than between different humans.

A veterinarian who incorporates acupuncture in her practice noted this variable. According to her statement to Dr. Hartman, "she can do maybe one acupuncture treatment on a horse and it would respond. When she does small animals, such as dogs with hip problems, *it takes much longer for them to respond* — and she has to do consecutive days for an extended period of time to get a response. With dogs, it took a lot more treatments."*

Why might this be?

"I have no idea," concedes Dr. Hartman. "One thing: a horse tends to be a highly nervous animal, and maybe there's a higher energy. If you could measure the actual nervous energy running through a horse, I'd bet there'd be a higher amplitude — or strength — of the actual conductance of energy through the nervous system, would be my guess."

As a Reiki therapist, you need to be cognizant of how the animal you're treating is assimilating the flow of energy — since it might vary more than you are accustomed to if you've only worked on people.

And as part of the awareness, *let the animal communicate to you what it needs.*

"Virginia was fond of saying how animals seem *more* in tune with Reiki," remembers Dr. Hartman. "And my personal observation is that that *is* true. Not only are they most of the time very receptive to it, but also they will tell you when it's time — if you are in tune and paying attention — they will tell you when it's time to move, when they've had enough in that one position."

---

* Dr. Hartman continued: "Just an anecdote. She said the acupuncture points for horses go back 3,000 years. Then she showed the charts for dogs and cats. 'Unfortunately,' she said, 'these charts just go back a few years because they have to be extrapolated from human acupuncture points — because the Chinese *ate* their dogs and cats!' Incidentally, dog and cat acupuncture points closely coincide anatomically with human points; however, the point locations of horses do not."

> **"With all beings and all things
> we shall be relatives."**
> **— Sioux Indian precept**

This point leads to a fifth difference: *animals are more apt to cue than people are* when a position change is timely.

"In my early days of practicing the first-degree Reiki, I wasn't always adept at feeling the rise-and-fall," Dr. Hartman admits. "But I could *always* use the animal's cue when to move on."

Most often, that cue by the animal is restlessness.

"And when they are in acute pain, when you first start the Reiki there'll be more pain during the first few minutes when you start. And sometimes they'll object to that. And you have to get over that, either by hardly placing your hands on them (almost letting an air space) or ever-so-lightly leaving your hands on them and talking to them."

What procedure do you follow, once the animal is acclimated to your gentle presence?

"That is where starting with the Crown Position is always the best — because that's the calming position,"

the veterinarian advises. "And interestingly enough, that conforms with the acupuncture point for calming dogs and cats! Now for horses, it's right in front of the pelvis — it is a different position for horses."

Now that the animal's possible panic is assuaged, the Reiki treatment can proceed largely on the basis of what seems most comfortable to you and for the animal.

"Now you may want to face them and have your fingers pointing down the back, or you may want to come from the other direction," Dr. Hartman says from his experiential background.

"Some dogs and cats or animals may be so fearful that they will not want to face you. You might want to approach them looking in the same direction, so they can't see you but just feel your hand placement. So you just have to feel what's right for that particular case.

"I've done it both ways. For disk and back injuries, I always start with my fingertips pointing *down* the spine. That seemed to me to feel the right way to do it."

An adjunct to Reiki that the authors have found very beneficial to use with small animals, especially rabbits, is *aquatherapy*.

As this chapter is being written, we are tending a wild rabbit with an irreparably injured spine and paralyzed hind legs. Every other night we immerse this young female hare in a sink filled with tepid water and mild castile soap, working her legs in a very slow natural motion for several minutes.

The benefits are many: 1) it keeps her fur and flesh clean and fresh-smelling; 2) it soaks off the urine and fecal matter on her fur and skin; 3) it prevents atrophying of the leg muscles; 4) it enhances the flow of energy through the damaged area of her body; 5) it aids her in kicking and stretching her legs as they rejuvenate; and 6) it actually entertains the rabbit by giving her a change-of-environment.

Believe it or not, this *wild* rabbit has never balked at the 'unconventional' handling. Indeed, she seems to enjoy it! (That she gets towel-dried and then Reiki therapy immediately afterwards for an hour might be a contributing factor, too.)

Don't be surprised to discover a sixth difference when working with animals: *dramatic change in personality and demeanor.*

Wild animals, unless the species is a predator, are generally thought to be skittish and wary around people (unfortunately with good reason). Domesticated animals, instead of being tame, can be frightened of people if abused or if aggressiveness is bred into the species. And injured animals, pet or wild, are apt to be unpredictably violent.

If this makes sense to you, be prepared for amazing surprises as you Reiki animals.

Consider the case of a pleasantly tempered cat which, hit by a car, suffered such a severe concussion it lost sight in one of its eyes.

"After the accident it had a definite behavioral change: very aggressive, very nasty, either it'd go after family members or be very reclusive," Dr. Hartman remembers. "It was definitely an aftermath of the concussion (of the brain damage).

"This is one *that really took dedication*, because the cat was so mean and nasty that I couldn't even directly lay my hands on it. What I had to do was capture it in a big bath towel (like a net) in its cage, scoop it up, and avoid any kind of environmental noises (which aggravated it). Then sit with it, concentrating on the head area and working back. I gave it three/four treatments in succession, then maybe once a week, twice another, once a couple of weeks ... because its owners were not willing to bring their cat back on a regular basis.

"But when they *were* bringing it in regularly, it got to the point where the cat would actually sit next to me in the lounge area on the couch, and I could do all its Reiki positions without the towel. That point was *definitely a decided difference* from before!

"I talked to the people a year later, and the cat is better than it was. It is almost completely normal again."

One more example is instructive. It involves an akita, a huge dog bred in Japan for palace guard dogs. The breed is very strong, very aggressive, very powerful, and can be very ferocious.

The akita that was brought to Dr. Hartman for treatment exemplified each trademark of its breed. With a vengeance! It proved to be a classic case of acute-care veterinary skill coupled with Reiki.

"Now this dog," he recounts, "eventually developed breathing distress and, to make a long story short, a *diaphragmatic hernia*. And all its internal organs were pushed up into the chest cavity. This dog actually required surgery to repair the damage — and it was a difficult surgery because of the massive damage. Even the entire liver was pushed up into the chest cavity.

"So what is significant about this, is the dog (with all that severe damage) went into *very deep shock*. I performed a three-hour surgery just to repair everything and get all the internal organs back into their proper places; we were administering emergency IV fluids, emergency drugs. That particular dog I spent the entire night with, literally ... from 11 o'clock in the morning when I started surgery until 7 o'clock the next morning.

"There's two interesting things about this case. Number one: because of the massive internal damage, this dog kept going into shock, going literally into respiratory and cardiac arrest three time. (We had him on oxygen the entire time.)

"About midnight, after massive amounts of replacement fluids and drugs just to keep it sustained, I felt I was losing ground. I felt that if I left that dog then, it would be dead the next day.

"So I started doing Reiki on it, and did Reiki for over two hours on that dog. I covered every position I could. Because it's such a huge dog, I could do most of the standard 14 positions on it.

"That dog was slipping in-and-out of near death all night. And when I was done after that two hours of Reiki, the dog looked bright, looked alert. I discontinued IV fluids. And it got up and walked out of its run! ... And I thought: 'I can go to bed!!'

"Nobody really knew how this happened. The staff knew I stayed all night and knew what I did medically, but one staff member asked if I did 'anything else' —

"That's another case where you're doing massive medical treatment and you're still not getting ahead of the problem; the animal is just holding ground or slipping away slowly. Reiki had to have done something — because I worked on that dog all night without gaining any [medical] ground ... "

The second point the veterinarian noted is this: the akita responded not only to the Reiki but, in a most uncharacteristic way, to the Reiki therapist as well.

"Interesting enough," Dr. Hartman recalls with amusement, "when I'd come into the kennel and walk over to its cage — now remember this is an akita, an aggressive dog which later bit every member of the staff and chased one member up on top of the refrigerator — I was the *only* one the dog would let come near. ... I was the only one who could touch him. This big mean aggressive dog would lay on its side for me to treat him."

What a satisfying and rewarding experience this must have been! Not to mention the astonishment with which the veterinarian's co-workers beheld this out-of-character bonding of the akita to its doctor.

But then, such "miracles" are expected when working with Reiki —

ANIMAL-SPECIFIC TREATMENTS

Dr. Hartman offers these specific pointers for indoor/tame household pets:

Hamsters: "I did do a Reiki treatment on a hamster. It was bleeding from a torn nail. Hamsters, like many small animals, like to squirm about, making them very difficult to do. At first, in my trying to hold its little paw, it fought. But eventually, in going back to it and being very gentle and being very slow with your movements, then it finally accepted it. And in a few minutes the bleeding had stopped, and it was standing on its foot again."

A very powerful form of healing to use on a small animal is to place your hands *sandwich style* on each side of its body.

Smaller creatures such as mice, guinea pigs, frogs and toads cannot be administered the full range of Reiki positions. So *cupping* them in your hands is the obvious method to give them Whole Body Reiki treatment.

Although their rapid respiration and metabolic rate should not worry you, because that is normal for smaller

The "CUPPING TECHNIQUE" yields complete whole-body Reiki for smaller animals with only one position.

animals, they will likely become noticeably quieter within a few moments. They seem to let go and relax — and then the healing is, literally, in your hands.

Birds: "If someone's trying Reiki with birds, be sure the wings are folded against the body in a very natural position.

"When you do Reiki on birds, *please by all means leave their sternum free to move* — because that is how they breathe. If you wrap your hands around the bird and put too much fingertip pressure on the sternum (the keel-bone), the bird will asphyxiate.

"So you basically want to do a *cradle-type technique:* just have the bird in your hand and by all means make sure the sternum is free, and make sure the wings stay flat against the body."

Cats - feline leukemia: "You definitely want to focus on the immune system there.

"You definitely want to cover the neck area, and the glandular area around the lower jaws (because that's where you find the lymph nodes). And then you want to cover the front aspect of their chest (because of the thymus glands there). Then you definitely want to cover the adrenal glands. Refer to anatomy sketches on page 91.

"With feline leukemia you want to cover the entire body. You do not need to worry about the limbs or the front aspect of the face. But starting from the crown and the corners (or angles) of the jaws and going back, you want to cover everything there.

"In a feline leukemia cat that is symptomatic (showing symptoms), with Reiki you may be able to alleviate some of the discomfort but you're not apt to change the progress of the disease. This would be just like people in the terminal stage of cancer: you can help with the pain but you're not going to take care of the problem. You're not going to cure the leukemia.

"But at the early onset, when it's important for them [cats] to develop an immunity, yes!"

What if you *think* your cat was exposed to feline leukemia?

Begin immediately by treating its whole body as described above, he says, emphasizing "covering the

kidneys and adrenal — which is important. I'd probably do the heel of the hand over the back, with your fingers of both hands going around so that you're covering the adrenal glands, the kidneys, the liver, the spleen all in one position. And that would be starting at — the landmark for this position would be at the last few ribs. That's where your thumbs would be placed. Just pay attention to the anatomy."

Cats - bladder infections: "Put your hands over the pelvic area on top — not underneath the belly, but on *top*. That's an excellent position for cats that have chronic bladder problems.

"You want to make sure your hands are covering the lower back and the pelvis, because that's where the nerves come off the spinal column that enervate the bladder.

"You do that *first*. Then you can sandwich your hands around the bladder itself to heal the bladder. But you first have to treat the nerves that enervate the bladder — since that's where the spasms of the bladder come from which makes the cat uncomfortable."

In general, continues Dr. Hartman, "I've found this technique very helpful for treating the lower back and pelvis for animals with bladder problems."

REIKI AND VETERINARIAN CARE

Reiki, naturally, is the perfect 'in-house' healing regimen: your pet gets extra doses of loving care and attention, while its body's energy is restored. Just as naturally, there can be times when the medical and surgical skills of a veterinarian are required.

Remember: when your pet becomes ill and requires the services of a veterinarian, ask questions and allow your veterinarian to *educate* you. Learn which organs, parts of the body, et cetera, are directly affected by or connected with the ailment — and don't hesitate to explain *why* you are being so inquisitive. Then use that information to determine the hand placements and times that will prove most effective.

And if you are fortunate to find a veterinarian trained in Reiki, such as Dr. Hartman is, your animal will have the *best* care that is available.

"For me with a busy practice," he says, "when medical treatment is not doing it and the animal is telling me that it's a fighter and wants to go on and to do whatever you can for it, those are the ones that are definitely susceptible to Reiki!"

But a willing animal, a Reiki therapist and a veterinarian cannot go-the-cure alone, Dr. Hartman asserts. The animal's owner or care-giver must understand that *patience and time* are part of the recuperative process.

"You *have* to have cooperation!" states Dr. Hartman of the owner/care-giver.

Cooperation can mean repeated trips to the veterinarian. "That's the problem with treating animals, at least on a professional basis: if you don't have cooperation it's going to be very difficult to do Reiki. They want the quick fix with the medicine.

"With people, when they start to feel better they will come back for more Reiki treatments. But people have to be pretty much tuned into animals and be willing to bring them back. And just to keep them in a hospital to do treatments several days in succession is difficult. So it gets to the point where it's not every case you can do Reiki. It gets pretty selective, just because of the environment that you're working under."

Thus when you begin Reiki treatment of a friend's pet, be sure the owner is aware that he or she *also* plays an integral and important cooperative role in the healing regimen.

If medications are prescribed for the animal, the Reiki practitioner has additional responsibility to consider. The veterinarian should be appraised of the alternative therapy being administered, and a collaborative routine established.

"If an animal is under the care of a veterinarian *and* is getting medical treatment — receiving medical treatment for their animal — there may be *some drugs that would be contra-indicated* when doing Reiki, that would dampen or minimize the effects of Reiki," Dr. Hartman stresses. "Cortisone, for example, definitely does suppress the immune system. It's a very useful drug and very important, but —

"Also, the *time of use* is important. When I did Reiki treatment on those dogs — when they came in with the spinal cord damage and acute paralysis — cortisone is definitely indicated to bring the swelling down.

"But — once you get the initial swelling down, you want to wean the animal off the cortisone and rely solely on the Reiki. You don't want to keep on high doses, even moderate doses of cortisone. As soon as you see any response, you want to wean the animal off cortisone right away!

"Antibiotics are generally safe," he notes. "I've never found any problem with antibiotics and concurrent Reiki treatment."

The veterinarian emphasizes one final admonition: "Steroids should *not* be administered with Reiki!"

Reiki Master Virginia Samdahl believes the marriage of allopathic medicine and Reiki would be wonderful because, as Dr. Hartman says, "there are some nice things medical drugs can do. But they can't do it all. And that's where the decided advantage of Reiki comes in.

"When you've done everything medically and the animal (or person) just cannot get 'over the hump', *Reiki becomes the decided advantage.*"

He paused, then recalled the case of the big akita: *"To this day I don't think that akita would have made it through the night. If I had left it up to trust in the medical treatment alone, the dog would not have made it."*

WILDLIFE

If you live in an urban area, your Reiki on animals will likely be limited to typical household pets. But if you live in the country, or on a mountainside as the authors do, injured wildlife and infant creatures orphaned or abandoned in their nests will eventually find their way into your hands — and heart.

Your work with wildlife will involve special demands, but will also offer a very special kind of reward.

First, these animals are not domesticated. They are, after all, *wild*. Unless very young, they will have instinctive fear of being handled by humans. Indeed the creature should not be handled at all, unless you can determine that it has been orphaned or abandoned by its patents. (The latter does happen.)

Ideally then, *second-degree Reiki is a natural for healing wild animals* because with second-degree you can heal without the need to touch.

Furthermore, if you conclude that it is appropriate to take the animal indoors for treatment and protection, remember *that* is another alien and unnatural environment for it to adjust to.

Hence treating wildlife has two inherent differences versus domestic animals. And you must begin your healing by recognizing what those differences mean to the animal's reality.

"The biggest factor," says Dr. Hartman, "would be

fear. And getting them over fright — which in most wild animals can turn to shock, which will kill them.

"So in dealing with wild animals, you may actually *not* want to go by-the-book, but instead *feel* which position they relax with the most. And that's where you start, and go from there."

As to the Reiki procedure to follow once the animal relaxes in your presence, Dr. Hartman offers this advice:

"In general with wildlife it would be the same as with dogs and cats: start out with the Head (or crown) Position, either facing or away, and cradling in your lap so you put your hands over the crown.

"Especially when you're dealing with any traumatic injuries, the back, or arthritis in the hips, definitely put your hands over the pelvic area on top — not underneath the belly but on *top*. This is very relaxing, too."

Once the animal's trauma or shock has abated, your loving touch combined with Reiki can begin the healing process. If the animal is very young, the vitalizing treatments will aid its survival and growth into adulthood.

Remember that the animal needs natural light to survive, along with your Reiki touch! (Indoors, *full-spectrum* incandescent or fluorescent lamps are strongly recommended.)

It needs shelter where it can feel safe and be comfortably confined: a large box or indoor wire pet cage works well, as does the bathtub. (If you have household pets, make sure they can't gain access to the wild creatures you are working with!) A small box into which the animal can retreat as a 'hiding spot' should be provided.

And it will need food. Now what does a small wild animal eat? Surprisingly *a lot!* Feeding the little critter can keep you quite busy.

The authors have successfully nurtured and returned to the outdoors infant rabbits, injured turtles and toads, plus Eastern gray squirrels so small they fit inside a shirt pocket. We feed them by using a baby doll bottle or, when they are older, a medicine dropper filled with this formula:

> 8 oz. whole milk
> 1 egg yolk
> 1 tbsp. white Kayro syrup
> 1 tbsp. vegetable oil
> 3 drops Poly Vi-Sol (or other multi-vitamin
>   supplement)

Gray squirrels can thrive on this formula for several weeks. However, our experience shows this formula can sustain infant rabbits not much longer than a fortnight.

Indeed, wild rabbits generally, and infant ones in particular, seem to be among the most difficult species to care for. Both physically and nutritionally.

A rabbit's spine is relatively lightweight and fragile. Since a frightened rabbit will violently struggle by powerfully kicking its back legs in lightning-fast movements, it can easily overextend its lumbosacral (lower back) region and thus fracture or dislocate its spine. Hence … you should *never* try to overpower a struggling

"Love the animals. God has given them the rudiments of thought and joy untroubled. Don't trouble it, don't harass them, don't deprive them of their happiness, don't work against God's intent."

**—Dostoevsky,
The Brothers Karamazov**

"Hear our humble prayer,
O God, for
our friends the animals,
especially animals
who are suffering,"
wrote Albert Schweitzer,
"and for those who
deal with them
we ask a heart of compassion
and gentle hands and
kindly words."

Expect to hear in return
the whisperings of nature,
maybe even a whispered
"Thank you!"

rabbit; rather, immediately release it, and re-approach it only when it has calmed down. Second-degree Reiki will aid in restoring calm. As will a soft-spoken demeanor, covering its eyes, and lightly stroking its forehead (which usually results in a hypnotic-like trance making the rabbit less prone to panic).

Many people who unintentionally disturb a rabbit nest think its infant bunnies have been abandoned by the mother, or will be abandoned because of human scent now on the nest. The former might be true; the latter unlikely, if you carefully restore the nest to its original appearance. (Because lactating mother rabbits often visit the nest only a few minutes daily — and then usually at night — to nurse her young, most people don't see the doe and conclude the bunnies have been abandoned.)

If the baby rabbits' eyes are open and bright, it's doubtful the nest has been abandoned. Remove the infants *only* if, after careful monitoring, you ascertain no activity from outside the nest and the babies show signs of malnutrition.

Now the *real* work begins! Raising orphaned wild rabbits is rarely a rewarding venture, to be blunt.

"The bacterial populations in a rabbit's intestinal tract are considered the most delicately balanced of any in all herbivorous mammals," say veterinarians Dr. Richard W. Woerpel and Dr. Walter J. Rosskopf, Jr, of the Avian and Exotic Animal Hospitals of Los Angeles and Orange Counties. "No other commonly kept house pet is as sensitive to dietary changes as the rabbit."

Any rapid change in diet — a problem compounded by the dispensing of artificial nourishment in the case of a wild rabbit* — easily upsets this equilibrium in an animal already under stress due to injury or environmental dislocation.

Consequences can be unpleasant. As Drs. Woerpel and Rosskopf explain: "Overgrowth of harmful bacteria [in the digestive tract] usually results in production of toxins that are rapidly absorbed into the rabbit's circulation, quickly causing illness and death."

If you choose to work with wildlife, and especially rabbits, be very alert to subtle changes in their hypersensitive metabolism. Here, Reiki will certainly benefit you … and the animal too, of course.

Success isn't guaranteed, but it *can* be achieved.

———————————

* Drs. Woerpel and Rosskopf suggest two formulas specifically for orphaned bunnies:

a) 1 egg yolk
    8 oz (240cc) canned evaporated milk
    8 oz (240cc) bottled water
    1 tsp (5cc) honey
    1 tsp (5cc) pediatric vitamin/mineral supplement.

b) 1 can Esbilac (Borden)
    1 raw egg (white and yolk)
    1 tbsp (15cc) Neocalglucon (Sandoz Pharmaceuticals) or similar liquid calcium supplement.

Physiological facts to know about rabbits: normal body temperature range = 101.5–103°F. … breeding age = 5–9 months (females), 6–10 months (males) … pregnancy = 29–35 days … litter size = 4–10 infants … weaning age = 4–6 weeks … life span = 5–10 years.

As soon as possible, wean your infant wildlife off this formula and onto solid food.

Young rabbits will eat grass — lots of grass. (Finding enough green grass during a Northern winter's snows to satiate the ravenous appetite of a year-old rabbit is, shall we say, challenging!) You can supplement their diet with carrots, kale, parsley, apples, rabbit pellets and "crunchie puffs" (the last two available at pet stores). And don't forget fresh water, often!

Squirrels will relish sunflower seeds, unshelled peanuts, chestnuts, cracked corn, and *especially* kiwis (fruit). Do provide a small branch for them to gnaw and climb on.

Kaeopectate should be handy, should the animal suffer sudden onset of acute diarrhea. Dr. Terry Reed recommends ¼ to ½ teaspoonful be administered each dosage, twice or thrice daily. (This dosage is for rabbits; adjust the dosages according to size of the animal being cared for.) For non-specific diarrhea, the addition of rolled oats or other fibrous roughage will hopefully ease the animal's distress.

If your wildlife patient is active, there's little more you can do and the prospects are good. However: if the animal is lethargic or maybe even suffers spinal paralysis — as does the wild rabbit the authors have tended for eighteen months — it will need you to administer massage, acupressure or/and aquatherapy in addition to Reiki so that its muscles don't atrophy.

One crucial factor to be wary about with hands-on healing of wildlife is *rabies*.

According to Dr. Hartman, infant animals aren't likely to have contracted rabies. But never take risks, especially if working with raccoons and stray dogs. Don't get bitten, or work with an unprotected open cut on your skin. Rabies is often fatal once symptoms appear, and treatment is painful at best!

Dr. Hartman offers these suggestions to Reiki practitioners who have the need to cue in on rabies:

"They're not going to have the availability of seeing saliva dripping from the animal's mouth and all that, but certainly any animal species that does something atypical for its species" is potentially rabies-infected.

"Like if you see a fox in a suburban area. Foxes are rather reclusive, they're nocturnal animals not out during the day," he notes. "Also: if the animal looks *especially gaunt and the abdomen is sunken in*. When an animal is close to the terminal stage of rabies, it will actually develop neuroglial paralysis — they can't swallow. That's why they show symptoms of saliva and frothing: they can't swallow. So when you see an animal that is extremely gaunt and sunken in the abdomen behind the ribs, that means it hasn't eaten in a couple of days — and there might be *a good reason for that!* So those are the obvious clues."

DEALING WITH 'FAILURES': WHEN REIKI DOESN'T SEEM TO WORK

Most sick animals will instinctively come to you for healing because they sense you can benefit them, although occasionally you might find one that simply will not respond to the Reiki.

"I had a dog almost refuse Reiki treatment," Dr. Hartman explains. "This was a dachshund, and it was in kidney failure — it turned out to be terminal kidney failure. For whatever reason, this dog refused Reiki treatment. You'd put your hands on his back, and he'd try to move away. And you *knew* this dog did not want the treatment!

"I definitely feel that they can feel the energy *much more intensely* than people do," he says about animals, and this is why some of them "will not allow or be conducive to the Reiki treatment."

As with people, not all animals can (or desire to) be restored to physical health.

Animals have their own time to physically transition when their life's chosen aim and purpose is completed, and they have the free will not to accept energy that would thwart their situation. Dr. Hartman agrees:

"People who have failures with animals or failures with wildlife," he cautions, "it's not necessarily that they're not good with the Reiki or anything like that. I think in the animal world you're going to have some that, for whatever reason, do not want to accept the Reiki energy. They don't want to get better. I think there are some unknown factors as far as whether or not the animal chooses to get better; whether or not it's a terminal problem. It's their time, and they want to die. I think that's the biggest factor: it's their chosen time to go …

"And the person has to realize that, if it's terminal, it is something that's gonna happen no matter if Reiki is done or not."

How can you determine whether the animal in your hands is open to healing or to its physical transition?

"When you start a Reiki treatment," answers Dr. Hartman, "you'll know pretty much right away whether or not the animal will accept it — and more so, whether or not it will be successful — just by the way they accept the Reiki treatment. And you can tell, if not right away then within the first few treatments — just by their attitude.

"So that's a precautionary note. They're going to have some failures, especially when working with wildlife."

But showing compassion to an animal can hardly be viewed as failure, regardless of the final outcome. Each effort by man to restore kindness and caring toward the animal kingdom is a contribution toward the healing of the planet.

LESSONS LEARNED WITH ANIMALS

You will surely learn much as you work with animals.

You are likely to become more sensitized to the transmission and acceptance of energies generally; to subtle cues and clues about the healing process. Of course, these insights garnered from working with animals will aid your Reiki practice with people too.

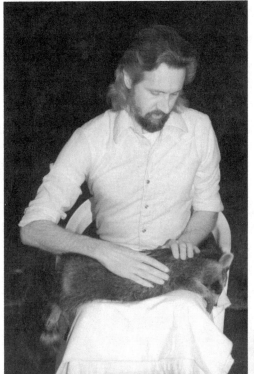

"In a world older and more complete than ours they move finished and complete, gifted with extensions of the senses we have lost or never attained, living by voices we shall never hear. They are not brethren, they are not underlings; they are other nations, caught with ourselves in the net of life and time, fellow prisoners of the splendor and travail of the earth."

—Henry Beston

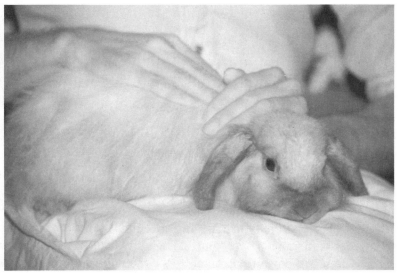

Beyond that, you will learn about animal intelligence and behavior. Ultimately, you become attuned to the range of consciousness found in non-human life.

The authors have heard hunters say innumerable times that all animals are alike; that is, dumb … that to anthropomorphize animals is childish, infantile, baseless and naive … that animals have no feelings and no individualized personalities and characteristics.

These are remarkable conclusions, considering they are based on observations made in a few seconds through the crosshairs of a rifle scope.*

Not only arrogant assumptions, these conclusions are *wrong* — as you, and anyone, who works intimately with an animal (especially several animals) will discover almost immediately!

Some species — including members within the same species — are docile, others aggressive; some playful, others languid; some will sit on your lap for hours to enjoy your stroking and Reiki transfers, others will give your lap "a minute of their time" (literally) and then want to roam the room — coming back to your hands when *they* (not you!) are ready to resume with touching.

Every animal is as different and individual as a person is. This you will come to know.

As you become increasingly aware of this fact in your work with Reiki and communicate your personal observations to others outside of the Reiki community, humaneness toward the Animal Kingdom — which should be man's attitude, rather than domination — shall resume global expression. Again.

And that is another gift which Reiki, and you, will give to this world.

---

* For example, James S. Biery, past president of the Pennsylvania Federation of Sportsmen's Clubs, writing to *The Patriot-News* (September 6, 1989): "The concept of humanizing an animal mentality and attributing human-like behavior to members of the animal kingdom create [sic] serious doubts about whether some of the individuals have come to understand the realities of the natural world. While it has always been known that children will personify animals, once the mind matures [?!] that belief is lost — "

9
Reiki Recipes

REIKI SLAW

1 head green grated cabbage
1 head grated cauliflower
3-4 large raw beets (omit rather than use canned beets)
5-6 celery stalks, chopped fine
onion or onion powder (if desired)

Mix with hands, add choice of dressing. Eat one cup daily. Excellent for the intestines.

BLOOD REPLENISHER

1 head large white or green cabbage
1 large bunch of watercress
3-4 large raw beets (omit rather than use canned beets)
4-5 stalks celery

Juice the above ingredients together. Serve this mixture as the *entire* diet for 7 days, drinking whatever quantity is desired. Then resume a varied, nutritious dietary plan.

SOY MILK

Measure 1 cup dried soy beans into 4 cups of water. Let stand 8 hours (or overnight). Boil, and skim off the "fuzz." Simmer 2 hours and then remove heat. Blend 1 cup of beans* with enough water to make 1 quart. Two cups of soy milk are equivalent to 1 lb. of beef steak.

* Soy powder may be substituted, making sure it has no additives or preservatives. Available from organic food stores; also Walnut Acres® Organic Farms (PO Box 8, Penns Creek, PA 17862-0008. Phone 800/433-3998).

WHEAT GERM ZUCCHINI BREAD

1 cup wheat germ (any kind)
½ cup sunflower seeds
1¼ cup whole wheat flour
3 tsp. baking powder
½ tsp. salt
¾ cup grated zucchini
⅓ cup honey or maple syrup
¾ cup milk
1 egg
chopped sprouts (optional)

Combine above ingredients, and bake in a greased pan at 375° for 30-to-35 minutes or until knife comes out clean when inserted. Let cool in pan.

CORNMEAL BREAD

2 cups unbleached white flour
2 cups gritty yellow cornmeal**
5 tsp. baking powder
2 cups honey
½ cup safflower oil
½ tsp. salt
2 large eggs
2 cups sweet or sour milk

Preheat oven to 375°. Mix all ingredients well; mixture will be thin and slightly lumpy. Pour into 2 heavily greased pans. Bake until loaves are springy-to-the-touch and a knife inserted in the middle comes out moist. Serve piping hot with butter or honey.

** Cornmeal, stone-ground by water power, is available from Pigeon River Milling Company, Pigeon Forge, TN 37863; Old Mill of Guilford, RR 1 Box 623, Oak Ridge, NC 27310-9801; and Burnt Cabins Grist Mill, Burnt Cabins, PA 17215 (717/987-3244).

霊気 10
Equipment for Reiki

Reiki healing really requires nothing more than a Reiki therapist and someone (or thing) to treat.

However, a table specifically designed for body contact work such as massage, rolfing, acupressure therapy and, of course, Reiki is often used for the comfort of *both* the client and healer.

"Get one so your knees will go underneath," recommends Mrs. Samdahl, "to avoid the need for chiropractic yourself."

On the following pages are suppliers of equipment suitable for use in administering Reiki treatments:

the natural choice

for Reiki Therapy

travel covers

headrests and face rests

Colorado Healing Arts Products
PO Box 2247-R
Boulder CO 80306-2247
(see display ad on facing page)

Earthlite Massage Tables
120 N Pacific St Ste L7
San Marcos CA 92069-1269

Living Earth Crafts
429 Olive St
Santa Rosa CA 95401-7022

Oakworks
21300 Heathecote Rd
Freeland MD 21053-9601
(see display ad this page)

Pisces Productions
6979 Baker Ln
Sabastopol CA 95472-5023

The Touching Company
PO Box 10532
Portland OR 97201-0532

HARMONY · HEALTH · HAPPINESS · REIKI

"Man can no longer live his life for himself alone."

— Albert Schweitzer

霊気

11
Reiki
Affirmation

Metaphorically, the universal life energy that flows through the application of Reiki ... is like the stream choosing its own path and rate of flow as it cascades naturally and gently to nourish and invigorate that which it touches;

... is like the softness of a woodland breeze;

... is like the strength of majestic trees that can be resolute yet flexible;

... is like the serenity and peacefulness of Nature in balance — each aspect perfectly complementing and meeting the needs of all else.

But what is Reiki, the energy and the system?

Reiki Master Virginia Samdahl describes it in the following affirmation:

REIKI is God's love in its purest form.

It is completely unconditional.

It demands nothing of the giver nor of the receiver.

It propounds no creed or dogma.

It requires no specific belief in the supreme being or in reiki itself.

Used in its traditional form, as developed by Dr. Usui in the Usui System of Natural Healing, reiki heals the body and emotions, bringing them into balance and promoting health, happiness, prosperity and long life.

118

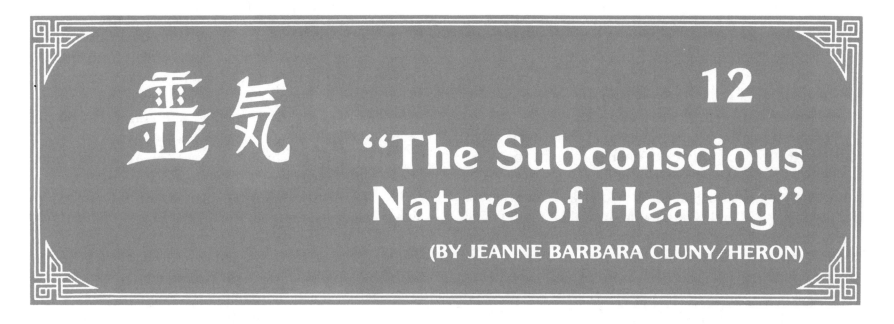

12

"The Subconscious Nature of Healing"

(BY JEANNE BARBARA CLUNY/HERON)

What follows is a verbatim transcription of a dissertation delivered April 7, 1981, by a consciousness-being identified as Heron through the altered consciousness of Jeanne Barbara Cluny.

The authors have enjoyed a fruitful association with Ms. Cluny, finding insights presented through her to be provocative and illuminating.

We have therefore chosen to include this rather unique statement — published here for the first time — about the interaction of energy, consciousness and healing for your own consideration and evaluation.

… If I see that you are deeply amenable to what is brought forth, then I shall continue.

By amenable I do not mean you must accept without equivocation all that I shall bring forth — for as you know, you must always take what is brought forth as well as you can and come to your own deepest intuitive conclusion.

This is *always* understood in whatever information is brought forth in the altered state [of consciousness].

Now many times you cannot ascertain, you cannot prove what is brought forth. New facts come forth and you must need be very, very discriminating because what is brought forth can be deeply disconcerting to yourself.

Now what do I mean by "disconcerting"?

You shall need to always evaluate your own emotional stance before you can evaluate what is brought forth.

Now why is this so? Why do I not simply…bring forth a more elaborate dissertation upon what you already know? I, Heron, cannot allow myself to compromise myself, so I must bring forth my truth (what is within my knowing).

Now my experience encompasses every known detailed truth concerning the human body. It has been my forté and my quest and my discipline since I came forth into what could be called the Basic Real Universe; the reality that Is. So in the vernacular, it could be said I have spend aeons of time studying the human body (among many other considerations). The human body is my deepest joy. It is because I have not experienced being human.

So the human body represents to me a profound miracle that is ever being created.

So what I bring forth will be deeply controversial, and I must explain this in a light way.

Many have taught you ways and means of using energy to provide a healing stance. I, myself, applaud what has been brought forth.

But what has been brought forth must need be very simple. For we know we're dealing with human beings who are basically dwelling in fear about many unknown mysteries, as it were.

The mysteries are ascertained. And yet, although it is known certain mysteries exist within the Universe, still man is basically fearful. And this is natural. So what was brought forth … barely skims the surface of what really occurs within the art and discipline of healing.

Many who are working with energy under the auspices of those who have presented information are beginning to realize that something indeed is missing. This was understood from the beginning. We ourselves must work with human beings knowing full well that human beings create their own reality.

Knowing that you create your own reality, we must work with the reality *you* create. Always remember this.

So many times you have been disconcerted by what has been brought forth by all of your beloved teachers. But the intelligences that belong to all who have presented to you are vast and so profound you could not begin to evaluate the reality behind the picturesque expressions that are brought forth for yourselves.

So when you need evaluate what is brought forth, always hold to yourself that we do have a deeper wisdom that cannot always be ascertained by yourself at a given time. But when you view the overall view from the perspective of successive years fulfilled for certain fortés wished to be brought forth, you shall see the deeper wisdom that is occurring at all times.

So I admonish you lightly to always hold to yourself a certain reservation that suggests, "Well, we cannot understand what they are about at all times, but we will hold to ourselves two main considerations. Those who speak forth bring to themselves the deepest constructiveness and understanding of reality. Also, we hold to the idea that even though this is so, we must be our own authority at any given time; we must keep our own self-respect and self-esteem intact at all times and yet we must look for the transcendent note in what is brought forth."

So what I bring forth does not negate what has been taught. What I bring forth cannot simply be a review of what has been taught, either.

What I shall attempt to bring forth this evening is what can be known at this present time in your development as human beings who are becoming more and more aware of the reality before them.

THE DIRECTION OF ENERGY

Now let us go forth and speak about energy.

This kind of energy we are dealing with cannot be seen with physical eyes. This kind of energy *can* be ascertained through the symbology brought forth through the inner senses. In this way you can see energy, and yet it is a symbol brought forth by the subconscious.

So when you think you see energy manifested or expressed through photography or your mechanical devices, in truth you do not see the energy. What you see is an agreement upon the part of many human beings upon a subconscious basis to see that they wish to see; to prove what they wish to prove. But in truth what is brought forth in each instance is an illusion.

Also, therefore, it is an illusion because you cannot see and cannot measure this refined energy. It can be seen through *symbolization* brought forth by the subconscious. When you see an aura — or what I prefer to call an "illumination" — you are seeing it with your inner sense of sight; it cannot be ascertained with the physical eyes.

But even there, a symbology brought forth so that you can relate to what is being real before you.

Energy can be felt. This is how you can ascertain that energy is working for you, that energy is present. Energy can be felt.

But the interesting thing I wish to bring forth here is that energy is deeply apparent at all times. For everything that exists is composed of refined energy. Everything is energy! It can be nothing else.

So you are energy dealing with other energy forces/manifestations. And everything you do, say, feel, think, is an expression and a manifestation of this energy. It is very refined, it is real; it is felt, it is sensed. And yet it cannot be seen — it cannot be ascertained in that way.

Now, one of the laws that govern energy in this illusional reality as far as the healing process is concerned is simply this:

You cannot direct energy to another energy field reality being [a body] and have it (shall we say) accepted if the recipient does not agree upon the conscious level, the unconscious level and the subconscious level. And all three levels must be in agreement before one can direct energy to another successfully.

When energy is directed to another energy field reality being — a body — when it is directed it shall simply, as

121

you would say, bounce off the recipient. And I bring this forth.

Now it's been said that if this occurs, the energy is then redirected to the one who has intently sent the energy. This is not so. The energy then goes forth into infinity. It does not boomerang, as you say; this does not occur. Energy goes forth into infinity.

Now in order to direct energy in order to bring about an effect [which] suggests balance within a human body, you must have no doubt — *no doubt whatsoever* — that what you sent forth can be effective.

If you bring forth doubt, you immediately cancel the impending effects of that energy. What then occurs is an agreement between the sender and the recipient that a certain deep calmness shall be felt. For that is always the agreement.*

Let me state it again. If the sender does not hold to himself the deepest intent and the deepest faith in his ability to direct energy to one who apparently wishes for energy, the energy shall simply be fragmented and go forth into infinity. If the recipient truly does not wish for the energy to come forth within his energy field reality, then he shall simply block it and once more the energy shall go forth into infinity fragmented.

When the sender wishes to direct energy at a given reality field — a body — and holds no doubt in his ability to bring it forth, and when the recipient holds no doubt within himself and truly wishes for a balance upon the conscious, unconscious and subconscious levels of his being, then something may occur.

But what occurs in truth is *the sender knows quite well the recipient in a sense shall call forth from himself his own ability to direct energy to himself.*

It is an agreement upon the unconscious level. "I send it to you, and I will support what we both know. So now you can put forth your own power to heal yourself." It's an unconscious agreement.

---

* Mrs. Samdahl remarks:

"This, in my experience certainly holds true for most 'conventional' healing methods. But with Reiki, the conscious intent of placing the hands on the heal seems in some way to supersede this problem. I do not know why, but it does.

"Reiki also seems to reach some level in the healee, by-passing any doubts on any level within them. Perhaps it relates to faith as a grain of mustard seed that the Great Teacher referred to. As I say in my classes, 'If you have enough faith to reach out and touch, Reiki turns on and healing takes place.'

"I believe this puts Reiki on a higher plane than that discussed by Heron, for it takes human ego completely out of the situation and makes the healing situation completely impersonal, which in my opinion it should be. I recognize and affirm that we all need a good strong ego, or we are mighty sick. However, egotism is a stumbling block which many healers continue to fall over, no matter how loudly they proclaim 'I am only a channel!' I feel *that* is the greatest professional illness.

"Certainly in the so-called faith healing methods that I know, Heron's statements are true without question. But I do not find doubt to be true in Reiki."

Now when these dynamics do not occur between two individuals, than another agreement is set up:

"I shall send the energy to you and you shall gather it to yourself. But what we shall probably both agree to do — if we are both feeling in this manner — is [that] *I* shall feel rewarded and *you* shall feel calm." It is an agreement.

Does healing take place? No. It may appear so for the moment, for both wish for it to occur. But healing does not take place in the deepest sense of that word.

But a certain light healing, if you wish to use the word healing (I prefer the word "balance"), this might occur.

What shall be brought forth is the agreement: "When you direct energy to me, then all my aspectal memories shall simply dissipate from my being for the moment and I shall be deeply calm. And for that moment I shall feel balance within myself, for you have released me from my memory."

If truth be told, the individual releases himself from the memories.

However, since the dynamics are set up in a certain way that a certain imbalance is evident, then what shall occur is that after a short space of time the prevailing imbalance shall flourish once more within that energy field reality being — because there are deep and dynamic reasons for imbalance within human bodies. And they simply cannot be eradicated because one simply *wishes* to direct energy and another *supposedly* wished to be healed.

It is not that simple! What truly occurs is a deep bond of calmness and repose and a certain peace with the individual. It is agreed upon beforehand.

But it is a beginning. It is a beginning.

MALADIES AND IMBALANCES

Why do human beings suffer malady? Why does the human body express imperfections? Why does it express certain deep imbalances? Why does it express the deepest manifestation of psychological disorders?

Well, there are many reasons why the human body allows itself to be maligned — for this is what occurs.

In a sense the body has its own consciousness: it's deeply aware and alert at all times to what is occurring within that body. At the same time it could be said you have consciousness, as well, which does not depend on the body. This you know. Your consciousness does not depend on the body, for the consciousness can leave the human body.

And yet at the same time a certain dichotomy exists here, because the consciousness of a human being is immersed in the consciousness of the body. Because you are an energy field reality being, the consciousness that you are being is continually creating the body as it is being at any given moment. So in a sense you are not your body; and in another sense you are indeed the body expressing.

Why does the body choose experiences that suggest a deep malignment of itself?

Now there are many, many reasons why this occurs. Just as you came forth into physical reality to evolve in consciousness — to mature and evolve and much, much more — now the body is given to you in a sense (and yet you create it in another sense) to mature in consciousness.

In the beginning, when the body was you (as it were), it was fashioned beautifully. It was the most complex and miraculous computer you can imagine. The body's intelligence was *profound.*

But over the aeons of time, man began to bring forth directive to his body.

Why did this occur? What caused it?

Allow it to be said there are many, many versions of this reality. At this time there are perhaps (in round numbers for yourself) seventeen versions — parallel versions — of *this* reality. And they are forever being recreated in certain ways.

But allow it to be said that each parallel reality decides upon its own experience as far as mass consciousness is concerned. It is its own experiment. Just as you come forth to experience your own experiment in intimate and personal ways, the mass consciousness also decides what it shall experiment with in a given reality.

This particular version of reality that belongs to you at this time decided to experience a certain experiment that would lead the body from its original state of being through deeply creative changes until mankind could once more bring forth — *upon its own authority* — the *original* pattern for a human body. This is your experiment.

So early man decided — consciously — "I shall bring reference points to my body and how it operates for myself." And this was the beginning where man began to bring directives to the human body.

Now when directives began to be given to the body, the body in its own turn follows the directives (although the body has a consciousness of its own). And this consciousness would allow the body to operate in a clearly balanced way most of the time — for this would be its theme: to maintain a balance. Still, it allows a directive that came forth from the consciousness to affect changes in its original pattern of being.

When this began to occur, the body began to alter itself following the instructions from the consciousness. The consciousness, as you know, creates the body at any moment. And so the body that began to be created expressed the deepest beliefs within mankind concerning his own human nature.

This was the experiment: *How would man create his own body when he was given full rein to interpret the reality around him as he created it.*

So what occurred is that man began to see the body as something that belongs to him but was deeply alien to himself and must be watched, monitored, and directed in every function of its daily existence.

So the living organism — the body — began in its own way to keep its balance even though man brought forth destructive directives to itself. This is mass consciousness.

And so, since the power of mass consciousness

was deeply evident, these beliefs began to be held in the deepest ways that did indeed suggest "My body cannot be depended upon to care for itself. It cannot know how to balance itself in any great way. So I must always bring my own authority to this human form that is my own."

Now in truth, in the deepest truth, the body can maintain itself at any given time. It can *always* heal itself, no matter how horrendous or debilitating a malady might be.

And yet it cannot occur at this time in your reality, for the mass consciousness beliefs are quite profound. And this is so.

Now what has this to do with the multidimensional history of yourself?

Throughout all these centuries of time — I prefer "aeons of time," but allow centuries to hold — man experimented with his body. So he brought into being within himself and his multidimensional reality all manner of imbalanced psychological stances concerning the body.

So what occurs in simple terms is that when you come forth into three-dimensional reality to express, you not only bring forth all those different themes that you shall work upon in a psychological way expressed in your physical reality but you *also* bring forth themes that belong to the body.

For instance, you may decide that "I shall work upon the theme Loyalty/Betrayal. I shall work upon the theme Discipline. I shall work upon the theme Compassion." What shall occur in your life is you shall continual-ly be confronted with situations that provide a certain dynamic stance where these qualities of being can be explored.

When you speak about your Aim and Purpose, many individuals think it simply means "I must come forth to do this kind of thing or that kind of thing in my own intimate way." And this is not so. You work upon historical themes; you work upon dynamic themes that belong to your multidimensional reality and have belonged to that multidimensional reality for what could be said thousands upon thousands of years. You simply take some of those themes that belong to your multidimensional being and decide to work upon them in this reality. So you are always working with World Themes.

The *body* has its own themes.

You may decide in one life to work upon the theme (as far as the body is concerned) that suggests "I must learn to bring the deepest discipline to myself, so that I may understand my own physical welfare in deeper ways."

Perhaps in many, many life expressions you maligned the body in the deepest ways. So you might work upon the theme, "This time I shall try to discipline this body so that I can understand the deepest wisdom of my body. I can bring forth new directives that suggest Welfare for this body."

Or you may decide to work upon the theme of Patience and Endurance. And so you shall gather to yourself those situations in this life that shall allow you to learn patience and endurance.

And they shall come forth through the body experience. For allow it to be said, you may have brought the deepest directives to the body that suggest the deepest imbalance. So you shall try to balance what was done destructively in other life expressions.

What is being said, is that you come forth to balance many many life situations that belong to your aspects — besides your own. In bringing about this balance in a psychological way, you also did undertake to bring the deepest balance to the physical body.

One man in a given lifetime may say, "In this life I shall not experience disease. I shall not experience severe accidents. I shall simply not experience anything horrendous that need occur to a body, for I am working on psychological themes. And I myself, being the self that I am, have gleaned enough wisdom so I need not learn more about body welfare."

This can occur.

But in most cases a man will decide — and bring it forth in his [life] script, as it were — that he shall indeed learn something more about his own reality through discrepancies brought forth in the human body. In other words, they have been called for and directed.

If a man decides to experience what you call cancer, then it shall occur for him. It need not occur for a long period of time. But he shall experience cancer, for it has been ordered by himself as an experience. Then he shall call into play, in a psychological way, all those inner dynamic processes that come together to support the disease called cancer.

The psychological stances of a human being work in harmony with the consciousness of the body to bring about a certain effect.

Now it is deeply understood by the self that it may wish to experience accidents to the body or disease in the body.

But what is also deeply important to understand is this: *Human beings must bring forth the* deepest *expression of their own reality forward at all times.*

It is a law, in a sense.

What I bring forth is deeply significant to yourselves at this time.

You have been so ordered — or so fashioned — that you must indeed express yourself in this reality so that you can know who you are. You can only ascertain and recognize your own reality through self-expression.

If this self-expression does not occur, you would go mad. This is the deepest fear of mankind: *the fear of madness.*

The deepest fear is madness. Because mankind knows, through his ancestral memory, that many times aspects of himself have gone mad because they could not express themselves as well as was needed to be. You have been fashioned to express yourself outwardly so that you can recognize your own reality.

Now this is so. But human beings cannot always express their truth in this illusional reality. You must always shelter your truth. However, there are ways to bring forth the deepest expression of yourself to yourself so that you can recognize who you are.

And this is the deepest beginning of emotional maturity.

But at this time man cannot bring it forth in any deep way because he is governed by the social myths of the day. Also, within the cultural stances of this illusional reality man has not been permitted to express his deepest feelings.

So what occurs is the *body* does take upon itself the full expression of whatever emotion you cannot bring forth. The body takes this upon itself to keep the deepest balance within the consciousness being. Otherwise you would go mad.

Now what is so insidious in your reality at this time is that many have lost touch with feeling.

So what is occurring upon a mass consciousness reality, is many many more human beings are suffering from the deepest physical imbalance. It must be so. Because you have reached a point in human development where the majority of man has indeed lost touch with the deepest part of his being: his emotional tone.

Now what I have brought forth does not in certain ways meet your expectations, this I realize.

But what I wish you to understand is that the body in its deepest wisdom knows what it is about. The consciousness deep within its self — the self that you are — *knows* what it is about. It has preordained many times for illness to be experienced, so that a greater maturity can be experienced in body, mind and heart. Also, the body must need express what you cannot. It keeps you balanced by taking upon itself imbalance.

So allow it to be said that these two main considerations must always be understood.

So when a human being asks for aid — "Heal me!" — he may say it upon the conscious level. Yet in truth he does not wish it for his own deepest and wisest reason. He may wish to experience what is occurring to him, even though the outward expression of himself denies it. The outward expression of himself may beseech for healing to occur, and yet the inner truth of that being denies the wish for healing at that given moment.

Now many times there is a deep cooperation between the subconscious, the unconscious and the conscious that suggests, "Well, I *do* wish to be balanced."

So what occurs is simply this.

The subconscious knows quite well that the existing self lives within an illusional reality and has created for himself a reality that abounds with the mass thinking of the day. So it directs in that self ways and means to bring to itself healing under the auspices of the existing experiment. Then a human being goes forth for a healing fully believing that it shall occur through outward means brought to himself.

In truth, it does not. The subconscious has directed the self to heal itself. But it must be done under the auspices of the prevailing experiment, which suggests healing must come from the *outside*. So there is an unconscious agreement between those who heal and those who come forth to be healed, that this is so. It is unconsciously known.

When you go forward to the medical profession

and ask for healing, it is understood upon an unconscious level that what is going to occur is a certain play (which is deeply significant in its illusional reality). The medical profession comes forth and brings all that it knows (can ascertain) at any given time in history and expresses what it knows to the patient, knowing full well that the patient shall heal himself. Upon the unconscious level this patient knows quite well that this is a charade, and that he must need heal himself. And that the very fact he has come forward to the medical profession suggests that healing *has* begun.

And I, Heron, so state it. …

FOUR PRINCIPLES OF HEALING

Let me continue.

Let us speak upon the healing art as it applies to yourselves in intimate ways.

Let us first speak upon the ways human beings can bring the deepest balance to themselves through the directives brought forth by themselves.

Now if you wish to maintain a deep balance within the human form, *you must find ways to express yourself.* If you cannot express yourself to another, then you must do it alone.

This is the first principle.

The second principle. *If you find yourself suffering with a malady of whatever description you wish to label the malady, then you must need comply with mass consciousness thinking most of the time because it is your belief system.*

The third principle. *If you are deeply susceptible to what is brought forth by mass consciousness beliefs, then you must hold to yourself all those directives that are considered truths at any given time in your reality.*

The fourth principle. *If you do not hold to these truths brought forth by mass consciousness, if your mind and heart have completely dismissed those truths that seem self-evident in your reality, then you can begin to heal yourself.*

But you shall need to understand why you wish to heal whatever it is that you are experiencing!

If you find yourself experiencing the deepest kinds of human discrepancies, then be aware that your own psychological stances are deeply disordered. Then you shall need to begin to bring the deepest balance and perspectives to your psychological reality. You must need dismiss the disorders.

This is the first step within the healing process. You must begin at the first.

Now when you begin to work upon psychological disorders or discrepancies, the body immediately begins to bring the deepest balance to itself.

But in the process of bringing forth this rebalance to itself, it may allow itself to take upon itself various

128

minor discrepancies for a time. The body shall do battle against the existing psychological stance entertained by the entity.

Why does the body wish to do battle?

The body has learned to perform, to express itself, under those existing psychological stances and it becomes accustomed to those psychological disorders and has created itself along those disorders for ever so long. To begin to change your deepest disorders brings a deep reluctance to the body. So a battle ensues; defenses are set up by the body.

What kind of body defenses are set up?

The most prevalent defense (that could be called a minor malady) is the storage of water. It is the prime cause of obesity. (It may not be logical to your senses, it may be not apparent that this is so; for what I bring forth does not support mass consciousness. Yet it is so.) It is the strongest defense against change.

Since the human consciousness is always in a state of change in one direction or another, the body continually defends itself primarily with water. It derives its origin from a water-based reality. So water is deeply significant to a human being.

Other maladies may come forth — light discrepancies that could be called defenses. These defenses are the activation of all the numerous viruses that are within the body.

Defenses may be activated that suggest what I call minor maladies but perhaps you would call major maladies. Here I would list migraine headaches as a defense; intestinal problems, digestional problems; excessive fatigue, lack of apparent energy within the human form. To me, these are minor discrepancies/defenses.

Once you begin to bring the deepest kind of balance to your psychological stance, and if you maintain the deepest kind of integrity to bring about change and express yourself as well as you can, little by little your body drops its defenses and begins to perform in its own optimum way in time.

Now what occurs when you find yourself suffering from something that does not seem extreme, does not suggest medical services, and yet is deeply uncomfortable?

You wish to direct energy to bring about a balance. So what can occur?

You can direct energy using whatever terminology is comfortable to bring forth, allowing the main intent to be "I wish to bring a surcease of this imbalance within myself." This is the intent.

So you may use words to direct energy.

What shall occur?

The subconscious already knows. The subconscious is aware of what the self wishes to bring about. The self is aware of what the outer expression of the self wishes to be about. Now if the outer self is in harmony with the inner self, then what shall occur is a certain surcease of the imbalance may occur most of the time.

Why is this so?

Well, this experience has already been directed through the subconscious process to the self. So in a sense this is your experience, so it shall occur. (This does not negate what I have brought forth before.) What occurred once more is a set-up. It has already been decided upon that this shall occur this way.

But what *truly* occurs?

When you direct the energy, you dismiss from your consciousness those *aspectal memories* that brought forth that very imbalance within your being. You dismissed the aspectal memory.

Now what occurs when you dismiss the aspectal memory is [that] a certain deep calmness comes forth. In that calmness, you release emotion. It occurs in that way.

Think about it. You direct the energy and you wait for something to occur. If you really believe and have no doubt that something shall occur, then something shall occur.

But *what* shall occur?

What occurs is the dismissal of the memory, bringing a calmness to the consciousness. When a calmness is reached, the feeling is released. Which, in turn, dismisses even more aspectal memories that came together to cooperate to bring forth the imbalance in the first place.

What occurs when two human beings come together, one who wishes to practice the healing art and one who wishes to be the recipient?

Again, it is a set-up. It is known unconsciously and subconsciously that something is going to occur: two people are going to bring forth a transaction with energy.

. How valid is that transaction being?

In many ways, it's a deeply valid transaction —

something *does* occur: both agree to bring a certain release of aspectal memories for a short period of time. The aspectal memories of both individuals are dismissed through the physical interaction of two individuals.

Let me state it this way.

Two individuals come together knowing full-well a transaction shall occur between them. This physical experience called into memory many aspectal qualities for both. One shall remember in the deepest way being the healer (perhaps) and one shall remember in the deepest way being the recipient of healing energy (so-called). Both bring forth historical memory.

These historical memories allow for certain feelings to be expressed between both, under the auspices of certain prescribed directives that are brought forth.

When this occurs, it is already known that a deep calmness shall prevail between both. One shall be able to say, "I have brought it forth for you." The other shall be able to say, "And I am deeply appreciative that you have allowed me to see that I can do it myself."

Both have dismissed those aspectal qualities of being that suggested the set-up in the first place.

Then what occurs is a deep calm, most of the time.

With the calm comes a release of emotions. When the emotion is released, even more aspectal memories are dissipated from the consciousness of both. In a sense, both are healed.

But the healing under the most-time circumstances is simply a healing (as it were) between two consciousness-beings. It is a healing, in a sense, because it brings a balance for both. It brings a psychological balance. It brings a certain deep healing, of something having been settled between two individuals. And this can occur with a group, as well.

So what is really occurring is deeply complex and profound, and deeply intimate between the sender and the receiver.

And yet in truth, what was wished for in the deepest ways — a physical healing — may *not* come about because this is not the agreement and this is not part of the set-up.

PRINCIPLES FOR DIRECTING ENERGY

Now let me go forward and bring more useful information to yourself:

◆ *Do not direct energy in an indiscriminate way.* What occurs if you do, is you send it forth fragmented into infinity.

◆ *Do not direct energy to another unless they ask for it.* And then be deeply discriminating with the use of energy.

◆ *Do not assume that another human wishes to be healed — even though he says he wishes to be healed.* You can ascertain the sincerity of another human being by the feelings that are invoked within you. You can sense it; you can sense whether a human being wishes to bring forth a set-up.

◆ *You can use energy every moment of your life.* And you do it without thinking about it, and so you have no doubt.

When you raise your arms you use energy, and you have no doubt that the arms will be raised. And so it is. But when you consciously wish to direct energy for whatever reason, you bring forth doubt.

◆ *When you bring forth doubt, the energy is completely dissipated.*

Should you practice using energy, even though there is doubt?

I, Heron, bring this forth: indeed you may practice! But always hold to yourself the deepest acknowledgement that what you are about is of supreme importance.

And although there is an endless supply of the creative force of energy available for your use, still you must bring the deepest respect for what you bring forth to yourself or others.

Doubt there may be, but if it is mingled with the deepest respect for what occurred, then that energy (which may be fragmented into infinity) is in a sense re-directed towards the Eternal Source. It is not lost. And in a sense it provides for its own goal: to go forth from whence it came.

Now I, Heron, have spoken to you and have brought forth all I wish to say on this subject this evening.

Now there are deeper complexities to be understood. But before you can comprehend the deeper complexities, you must bring to yourself a psychological stance that can support no available reference points.

Do bear in mind — and I speak for all who come forth to you as teachers — that what is brought forth to you is brought forth with the deepest respect and esteem for your being. What is brought forth for your knowing is brought forth through yourselves, with the deepest respect and understanding for your state of awareness.

Although the reality of what is being is infinite in its complexity and must reach a point even for yourselves where there are no existing reference points, still we can speak to you in ways that will not assault your senses. So we must speak in ways that allow you to have certain reference points ... that suggest the existing self (that you are being, ensconced in this illusional reality) cannot allow itself to go forward into realms of knowledge where there are no reference points until the self that you are feels [that] the outer expression of yourself holds a deep security.

So the self that you are, all of you, is deeply wise. It knows how much it can hold to itself at any given time. The self that you are is deeply respected by ourselves, so we cooperate with the self that you are.

We would wish to bring to you, in time, experiences in the psychological reality of your being where no reference points can be brought to the information brought forth. This is why the frequencies are being changed — so information can be brought forth through yourselves where your reality must needs transcend; must bring to itself a transcendent state so that you *can* understand reality beyond what you presently know ...

Know that the time is coming for those such as yourselves to go forth beyond this space of reality, and bring the deepest transcendent awareness once occurring to yourselves. And what is occurring is the reality of your being.

I am enjoined by many at this time to bring this forth to you, so that you may understand intuitively that for those who wish for it, it shall be. It shall come forth.

But we shall not assault your sensibilities, but shall bring it forth little by little. It is a mutual cooperation between the self that you are being, and ourselves. It is a mutual act of recognition — that recognition that suggests the loving oneness of all that is created. ...

Additional Notes

CHAKRA ENERGY BALANCING

"In a Reiki treatment we cover every chakra," affirms Mrs. Samdahl.

These energy centers are vital to the healthy functioning of the person — physiologically, emotionally and, according to metaphysicians over the millennia, spiritually as well.

It is important, stresses Mrs. Samdahl, that these centers be closed at the conclusion of a client's treatment. Otherwise, she says, "they are wide open. Move over them up *and* down with the hands."

It is beyond the scope of this manual to discuss the chakra system. However, you might wish to discuss its subtle energies with your Reiki master, whose experience and sensitivity can offer invaluable insights.

Many books about the chakras are available, too. The classic reference is C. W. Leadbeater's *The Chakras* (Theosophical Publishing House). An inexpensive primer is Peter Rendel's *Introduction to the Chakras* (Samuel Weiser). An excellent study which includes recent (1989)

scientific and medical evidence for the chakras is Rosalyn L. Bruyere's *Wheels of Light – A Study of the Chakras, volume 1* (Bon Productions).

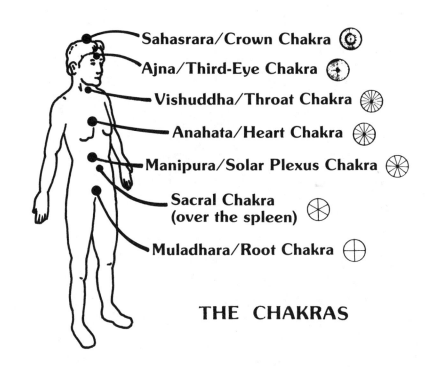

Sahasrara/Crown Chakra

Ajna/Third-Eye Chakra

Vishuddha/Throat Chakra

Anahata/Heart Chakra

Manipura/Solar Plexus Chakra

Sacral Chakra
(over the spleen)

Muladhara/Root Chakra

THE CHAKRAS

MUSIC, COLOR AND REIKI

People who claim that there is no evidence for subtle energies in the body, no chakras, and no reason to believe any method other than the Western-style medical practice of drugs and invasive surgery can heal, are unaware of evidence to the contrary.

In 1979, for example, both authors witnessed a startling experiment which revealed the presence of "invisible" energies associated with hands-on healing. The experiment took place at The Arthur Findley College for Psychic Studies at Stansted, England.

Trevor Stockhill, an English electronics technician and researcher, had modified a video camera to record portions of the infrared and ultraviolet electromagnetic spectrum. These bandwidths are normally unseen by the human eye. (Certain people, however, *do* have ocular sensitivity to these vibrations which flank the visible light spectrum — giving them insight, literally, into a world that appears very different, and invisible, to the rest of us.)

Stockhill's sophisticated equipment then filmed the Brazilian healer Alberto Aguas doing a healing treatment on a woman. Several selections of classical music accompanied the procedure, including Albinoni's "Adagio in G Minor," and "Spectrum Suite" by Stephen Halpern.

The filming was done in total darkness. Not one lumen of light illumined the room during the healing.

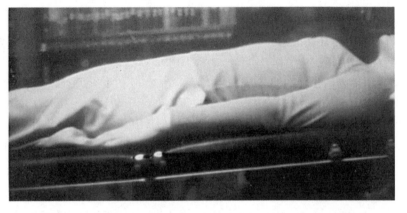

A: Patient lying prone, with lights on prior to healing.

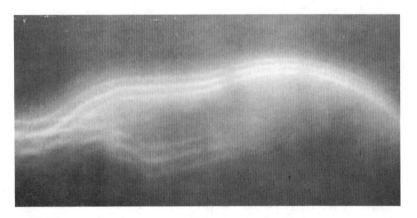

B: Same perspective as "A", showing ocularly invisible energies around the patient as recorded in pitch-blackness by Trevor Stockhill's specially modified video camera.

At the end of treatment by Aguas, the videotape — a virgin tape which was still sealed in its plastic wrapper until inserted into the recorder at the start of the healing session — was rewound and played back.

A standard video camera would have produced a blank image, there being nothing visible to record. However, something quite unforeseen mesmerized everyone.

The TV monitor revealed an extraordinary scene of rainbow colors coruscating around and through the client's prone body. From above, a kaleidoscope of hues "rained" down upon the woman. This curtain of light varied in intensity and brightness. It shimmered. It pulsated. It seemed alive. It was beautiful, and awesome to watch. At one point, streams of energy (composed of small balls of white light) appeared at the left edge of the TV screen and moved over the woman's body, then dipped into her abdomen. Colors changed in conjunction with certain tones and rhythms of the background music.

Aguas said at the session's conclusion that this healing had focused on a uterine ailment that the client was suffering. The videotape clearly showed streams of energy flowing into that area, though the many observers in the room had seen nothing in the black-dark room. In reviewing the videotape himself, Aguas noted that color shifts coincided with his channeling energy to different parts of the client's body.

This correlation between sound, color, and healing — the last being influenced and modifiable by the first two — has long been posited by pioneers in the medical community.

Edwin D. Babbitt, M.D., avowed more than a century ago that "Long repeated color therapy treatment *plus* proper diet produces wonders."

Dr. Oscar Brunler, a Scandanavian award-winning physicist and physician, investigated the impact of color (energy waves) on health. Before his death in 1952, he remarked: "Colors are far more powerful than medicine."

The influence of wavelengths of light on spontaneous tumor development has been quantitatively demonstrated in the laboratory by Dr. John N. Ott and others.

Perhaps Dr. N. S. Hanoka of India said it all when he professed: "Color therapy is universally applicable to all the ills to which the human flesh is heir."

But it was the Stansted experiment that uniquely *recorded* the rainbow of unseen energy present during — but *not* before or after — a healing treatment.

Reiki is an *ideal* healing regimen to study the interplay of sound and color and healing, because the therapist doesn't consciously need to concentrate on the healing *per se*, and therefore is mentally free to sense and examine what's going on elsewhere.

Hence you, as a Reiki therapist, might like to quantitatively and meditatively explore the efficacy of color and music upon healing.

As a guideline, you might investigate the healing attributes of color when shone on a client, as assigned by researcher Darius Dinshah, and how these correlate to Reiki placements. Refer to the chart on the next page:

COLOR	EFFECT	REIKI PLACEMENT
RED	Stimulates sensory nerves; builds haemoglobin; draws out infections	
ORANGE	Strengthens lungs and respiration; stimulates thyroid, stomach, and digestion; bone-building	
YELLOW	Stimulates motor nerves and muscles, the lymphatic system and intestines	
LEMON	Stimulates coughing to expel mucus; stimulates the brain and bone-building; mildly laxative	
GREEN	Stimulates pituitary; an antiseptic and germicide; general balancing	
TURQUOISE	Brain depressant; rebuilds burned skin	
BLUE	Stimulates pineal; relieves itching and fevers; encourages perspiration	
INDIGO	Stimulates parathyroid; respiratory and emotional depressant; arrests hemorrhages; sedative	
VIOLET	Stimulates spleen and white blood cells; muscular and lymphatic gland depressant	
PURPLE	Lowers blood pressure, heart rate and body temperature; kidney depressant; sedative; may over-stimulate sexuality	
MAGENTA	Equalizes blood and heart activity; emotional and auric stabilizer	
SCARLET	Stimulates kidneys, menstruation and heart rate; raises blood pressure; revitalizes sexuality	

The seven basic colors of the spectrum have been equated to sound octaves, as the chart below depicts. This presents another opportunity to explore the photobiology and sonic-biology of living organisms.

Perhaps you can discover an association with the basic positions of Reiki therapy.

Based on your experiential experience and sensitivity as a healer, fill in the Reiki placements sympathetic to color and sound as you determine them to be:

COLOR	NOTE	REIKI PLACEMENT
RED	C	
ORANGE	D	
YELLOW	E	
GREEN	F	
BLUE	G	
INDIGO	A	
VIOLET	B	

Your Reiki master may have more to say about the concepts introduced here. As will medical science, in time. All that is required for learning is the desire to know, and the initiative to ask questions.

Certainly much remains to be discovered — and *rediscovered* — about the energies of the human body ... and about the balancing — that is, healing — of those energies to assure maximum physical, emotional, and spiritual well-being for every person.

For every animal.

For the Earth.

Published references about color and health are many, and the following list is intended only as a starting guide for those who wish to explore this provocative and frontier-breaking field:

- Linda Clark's *The Ancient Art of Color Therapy* (The Devin-Adair Company, One Park Avenue, Old Greenwich, CT 06870)

- Darius Dinshah's *The Spectro-Chrome System* (Dinshah Health Society, 100 Dinshah Drive, Malaga, NJ 08328)

- The Fifth Kingdom's *Color Healing and Chromotherapy* (Health Research, Mokelumne Hill, CA 95245)

- Pat Kerr's research agency: Spiritual Science Institute of Canada, Box 524, Oshawa, Ontario L1K-7L9

- John N. Ott's *Health and Light* (Devin-Adair)

- Mary Anderson's *Color Healing – Chromotherapy and How It Works* (Samuel Weiser)

- Faber Birren's *Color Psychology and Color Therapy* (Library of Congress # 61-16266, Washington, D.C. 20555)

- Corrine Heline's *Color and Music in the New Age* (New Age Press, 4636 Vineta Avenue, La Canada, CA 91011); *Healing and Regeneration* (ibid.)

- Juliette Alvin's *Music Therapy* (Hutchinson & Company Ltd., 3 Fitzroy Square, London W1, U.K.)

Notes: _____

_____

_____

_____

_____

Notes:

Notes:

Notes: _____

_____

_____

_____

_____

_____

_____

_____

_____

_____

_____

_____

_____

"The very God-created soul is the medium of expression of health and disease and the purification or pollution of that soul is our ultimate personal responsibility here on Earth. . . . This health or wholeness is more than the mere absence of disease. It is the conscious touching of the kingdom within which God has planted, and it is living the affirmation that 'I AM me.'"

— Dr. Michael L. Connell,
"Spirit, Soul . . . And Medicine!"
Unity (July 1979, 27-8)

"So let us, in walking gently on the earth, leave behind a simple legacy —

HEALTH

HAPPINESS

HARMONY

REIKI

— that we loved the earth and had the courage to heal it, to save it for future generations."

To Heal Home and Humanity

About the Authors

LARRY E. ARNOLD developed an interest in human expanded awareness during his engineering studies at Lafayette College.

In 1976 he founded ParaScience International, a transnational network devoted to investigating and documenting the mysteries of man and planet least apt to receive serious consideration from scientists constrained by Conventionalism.

He is recognized internationally for his pioneering research in forteana, particularly the biophenomenon of Spontaneous Human Combustion. He has appeared several times on ABC-TV's "That's Incredible!" and NPR, lectured in the United States and England, and written for *Fate, Science Digest, Frontiers of Science, Pursuit* and *Esotera,* among others. He has chaired three Age of Consciousness conferences, two on the international level. His first book, *The Parapsychological Impact of the Accident at Three Mile Island* (1980), has been acclaimed as a "contemporary classic in reports on premonitions ... which will undoubtedly become required reading for parapsychologists in that it offers details and facts which are rarely researched in such depth or collated in a readable style."

SANDRA K. NEVIUS views life from an Earth-centered perspective and philosophy. In 1974, she became especially interested in healing as it pertains to animals and the balance of the planet itself. Seven years later, she chaired an international conference whose theme dealt with the many social and geophysical changes mankind now faces, and how to guide creatively those transitional forces into a *positive* transformation.

She holds a particular fondness and respect for the animal kingdom — her pet cats, Minnie and BeBee, and 100-lb labrador retriever Domino (imagine getting him up on the Reiki table!) are featured in Chapter 8 — and supports the work of a local animal shelter that aids injured wildlife in recovering their health.

A career engineer in the telecommunications field, Sandy also communicates by performing with a Near Eastern dance troupe, and teaches workshops which use Near Eastern dance as a means for women to discover, recover and express more openly their feminine nature.

VIRGINIA W. SAMDAHL is the first Occidental to attain Reiki Mastership in 2,500 years — making her eminently qualified to serve as consultant to the authors.

For many years she was involved in the study and use of psychic healing and prayer healing groups, but sensed there was a better way to heal. That way came in 1974 when she was initiated into the Usui Shiko Ryoho method.

Virginia retired from certifying Reiki therapists in 1989, though she continued to offer her experience and love in support of Reiki, and healing generally. About the joys of Reiki, she says: "I believe that there is only one great Creative Force in the universe, which I call God. It is from this source that the universal life energy is made available to us; for in order for us to be whole and to perform God's purpose for us here, we must be well. He has made this energy available to us so we can be as He meant us to be: perfect in body, mind and spirit."

For a full biography, read Barbara D. Lugenbeel's 1984 book, *Virginia Samdahl: Reiki Master Healer* (Grunwald and Radcliff Publishers, 142 W York Street Ste 605, Norfolk, Virginia 23510-2000).

Mrs. Samdahl made her earthly transition on March 4, 1994. Her dedication to healing and to living fully touched so many, and her loving presence endures through her friends and, of course, through Reiki itself.

"It is when you give of yourself that you truly give." — Kahlil Gibran